NEW YORK'S 50 BEST

Places
to take
children!

ALLAN ISHAC

ILLUSTRATIONS BY
KATHERINE SCHULTZ

CITY & COMPANY
New York

New York's 50 Best Cover Concept
Copyright © 1995 by Nancy Steiny
Cover and text of Places to Take Children
Copyright © 1997 by Heather Zschock
Illustrations copyright © 1997 by Katherine Schultz
Creative Coordinator: Kristin Frederickson

Printed in the United States of America
Ishac, Allan.
Library of Congress Cataloging-In-Publication Data
New York's 50 best places to take children/Allan Ishac.
p. cm.
1. New York (N.Y.)—Guidebooks. 2. Family recreation—New
York (State)—New York—Guidebooks. 3. Children—Travel—
New York (State)—New York—Guidebooks. I. Title
F128.18.I76 1997   917.47'10443—dc21   97-10911 CIP
ISBN 1-885492-30-8
First Edition

City & Company
22 West 23rd Street
New York, NY 10010

Publisher's Note
Neither City & Company nor the author has any interest,
financial or personal, in the locations listed in this book. No fees
were paid or services rendered in exchange for inclusion in these
pages. Please call ahead for up-to-date fees and hours. All area
codes are 212 unless otherwise noted.

Acknowledgments
I'm lucky. Lots of people helped me complete this book. First,
the many parents who spoke with me about great places to visit.
My agent, Susan Golomb, who cares about my writing and roots
for me. My friends at City & Company—Jennifer, Stephanie,
Kristin, Carlos, Heather, and especially Helene—who make it
feel like family. And most of all, Unni Benedicte, my friend, who
lived with me through the making of this book, who typed my
handwritten notes into the computer because I was afraid I'd lose
them, and who looks at me with that sweet smile that tells me
everything is okay. You are such a gentle Viking.

To my nieces and nephews,

Amanda, Sarah, Zachary, Alex, and Max,

who have always reminded me to drop

my worries and make balloon animals.

And to Elfie, who has been there

from the beginning.

Contents

10 MORE GREAT PLACES FOR KIDS...Just For the Fun of It!

Please keep in mind that this is New York and New York can get crowded. The locations in this book attract their share of enthusiastic children
and adults (particularly on weekends). Be alert to this possibility, and
leave an overcrowded location before you get frustrated. Or call ahead
to check on the best times to avoid large groups of visitors. Area codes
listed on the following pages are 212 unless otherwise noted.

Introduction

One of the things I love to do when I'm not busy writing books is make balloon animals. I always carry a fistful of balloons in my pocket in case I run into a young friend who would be thrilled to have a bubble mouse or a rubbery sword.

After many years, I've come to recognize a pattern whenever I twist a balloon for a boy or girl with adults standing by. The moment I finish the sculpture and hand it to the child, a parent inevitably remarks, "What do you say?" prompting a polite and reflexive "Thank you." What parents never realize is that I've already been thanked a thousand times over by the child's simple smile and delighted eyes. Those expressions of gratitude say so much more than words ever could.

I relate this story for a reason. I want to make the point that I did not pick the places in this book, children did. Not by the things they said (which are often unreliable because kids are trying to please hovering parents), but by their reactions. These can be trusted, and children have responded to the locations in this book with dazzling smiles, wide eyes, infectious laughter, boundless energy, and endless enthusiasm.

As you look through this book, you'll notice I have not listed hours of operation for any of the fifty places. That's because opening and closing times change often. Always call ahead for up-to-the-minute information and a schedule of special events for your children. Also, you'll find a note on the **Ideal Age Group** which is based on my observations of children visiting the fifty locations. These are suggested ages which will vary, just as children do. Ultimately, you must be the final judge of whether a particular place is appropriate for your child.

Also, every location description ends with a **Cool Kid's Corner**. This is my special note written specifically for children, and I ask that you read it to your child if he or she is unable to do so.

One last thing I've learned. Children want to play and have fun and go on great adventures, but more than anything they want to do it with you. Even if it's just *watching* them play—showering them with as much praise and attention and adoring looks as possible—you will have given them plenty. Forget about the warnings of our own parents' generation that all this love and admiration will go to a child's head. If it does, good—it's his or her best chance to grow up with some success in life.

Now, let's go have some fun.

Alice in Wonderland
Sculpture

Address: Central Park near Fifth Avenue and 74th Street
Ideal Age Group: 2 to 7 • Admission: Free

I f you've bought into popular arguments about computers and television and our high-speed, technoculture affecting a child's ability to enjoy the slower, simpler pleasures of life, let me present the Alice in Wonderland Sculpture.

There are no bells or whistles here, no buttons to push, no flashing lights, no microprocessors, not a sliver of fast-paced movement anywhere. It's about as low tech as you can get. Yet, everyday, children pull off the information highway to make an enthusiastic pit stop at this delightful sculpture— a virtual city landmark that's been drawing kids like a big bronze magnet for more than thirty-five years.

To be perfectly honest, I never much liked Lewis Carroll's *Alice in Wonderland* story as a child—too convoluted and weird. But you don't have to appreciate the book to enjoy this sunswept, south-facing sculpture. Just one glimpse at the ten-foot tall Alice astride her giant toadstool—surrounded by cartoonish, fictional characters from the story— and every fiber of a child's body shouts, "Climb!" I've even seen two-year-olds bound out of their strollers to explore the underworld of Alice's mushroom forest.

Sculpted by Jose DeCreeft, this memorial was a gift from philanthropist George Delacorte to his wife, Margarita, who, according to the dedication plaque, "loved all children." If there's any question that all children love her sculpture, just examine handholds like the Cheshire Cat's ears, the mouse's tail, the rabbit's pocket watch, and Alice's extended right arm—all burnished to a bright bronze shine by the sweat and oil from thousands of eager little hands.

I must confess, the temptation to climb into Alice's broad lap and rest my head against her bosom overcame me. A few five-year-olds stared and wondered why—but Alice didn't seem to care.

A cautionary note to parents: A favorite challenge for children older than eight seems to be a fast ascent to the top of Alice's head, where they hold onto her hair bows like reins. This looks a little risky to me, especially since the sculpture's base lacks that "soft fall" rubbery surface showing up in so many outdoor playgrounds these days. Bronze hurts when your head hits it. I'd keep an eye on kids of all ages.

COOL KID'S CORNER: Here's a fun game for children under six: see if you can find the lizard under the big toadstool, the caterpillar on the old tree, the squirrel popping out of his tree hole, the little snail, and the Style 10/6 card in the Mad Hatter's top hat.

American Museum of Natural History

Address: Central Park West at 79th Street • **Phone: 769-5100**
Ideal Age Group: 4 to 12 • **Admission: $7 adults/$4 children**

Environmentalist Rachel Carson once wrote, "And then there is the world of little things seen all too seldom. Children, perhaps because they themselves are smaller and closer to the ground than we, notice and delight in the small and inconspicuous."

It is precisely this wonderful quality about children that makes visiting the American Museum of Natural History with them such a pleasure. You're pointing out the tall, lethal-looking horns on a herd of gemsboks, while your five-year-old is staring at a hidden snake in the grass. You're fixated on the rippled muscles of the big leopard, while your child wants to know if the little black pig is going to be eaten. It happens every time—just when you think you're going to wow them with the big attraction, kids catch a subtlety that breathes new life into a diorama you've seen fifty times. Through a child's eyes, you get to see all the little stuff, the details you might never have noticed walking through this mammoth museum alone.

This isn't to say kids won't love the really BIG exhibits.

In fact, it's the towering Barosaurus and the dagger-jawed T-rex, along with the rest of the incomprehensible dinosaurs, that totally mystify and marvelize children. If these fearsome fossils look colossal to you, just imagine what they look like three feet below you. One reminder though: the immensely popular Dinosaur Halls will bring you and the kids back again and again, but other families have caught Jurassic fever, too. Get here just after the bony beasts have had breakfast and your visit will go much easier.

Although every dimly lit corner of these hallowed halls can seem slightly dangerous, you'll need little coaxing to get the kids enthused about the ninety-four-foot blue whale in the Hall of Ocean Life—eternally poised to nosedive through the floor. The dance costumes in the African Peoples Exhibit are also sights sure to elicit oohs and ahhs—look for Yahveh, a marvelous costume that's a cross between Chewbacca, the Midas Muffler Man, and a broom.

Other must-sees are the four Ecuadorian shrunken heads in the South American Exhibit (three human, one monkey), the giant Olmec Head with the pudgy face, those determined Haida Indians, still paddling their dugout war canoe after all these years, and the moon rocks (definitely not Swiss cheese) in the Meteorite Hall.

COOL KID'S CORNER: There's no question that Tyrannosaurus rex and other reptilian earth shakers were ferocious predators. For proof, just take a look at the Allosaurus fossil in the Dinosaur Hall. You'll see its bones deeply clawed during a savage fight. The horned Triceratops also shows evidence of a massive wound, this one a crushing blow to the left side of its skull. Ouch, I think that Stegosaurus just hit me.

Asphalt Green AquaCenter

Address: 555 East 90th Street at East End Avenue
Phone: 369-8890 • Ideal Age Group: 2 to 12
Admission: $15 adults/$7 kids for drop-in swim

One of my fondest memories of childhood was splashing around with my friends at the community swim club. It was nothing fancy, just a crisp, clean pool with a pair of lap lanes, a diving area, and a shallow end where we played Blind Man's Bluff and dove for pennies until the tips of our fingers turned to white raisins. That pool was cool.

New York City's public pools, on the other hand, have received some bad press lately for being generally unclean and unsafe. And because there are so few of these city managed swimming holes, they are overcrowded, too. What's a little fish to do?

I strongly recommend grabbing the swimsuits and nose plugs and anchoring the family at the best indoor pool in the entire city—the Asphalt Green AquaCenter. This contemporary complex was built from the architecturally significant shell of the former Municipal Asphalt Plant—hence, Asphalt. The Green relates to a regulation-sized, artificial turf soccer field that forms the emerald core of this handsome sports facility, and is available for free walk-on use.

The large, chlorine-clean aquatics area is truly a wonderland for water lovers, refreshingly painted in a get-you-in-the-spirit aquamarine blue. Asphalt Green has two magnificent pools—a fifty-meter Olympic-size pool that has been host to major competitions, and an eighteen-by-twenty-six-foot sister pool used for water babies classes and physical rehabilitation. The therapeutic waters of this smaller pool are kept at a toasty 88° F.

Parents are free to watch the family frogs from a dry spectator gallery overlooking the pools, but it's much more fun to get water logged with the kids, taking your belly flops and playing those dipping and dunking games. The AquaCenter also has kickboards and pool buoys, along with those brightly colored foam noodles that are the current craze. If your child is a serious water sprite, enroll him or her in the innovative swim school classes geared to every level from doggie paddlers to fearless backstrokers.

Besides a kid-sized basketball court in the refurbished asphalt plant building and an elevated indoor running track, Asphalt Green also has an excellent playground at the York Avenue entrance with rail-tie climbing apparatus and lots of room to run. I must also insist that you take any child under seven to the on-site Lenny Suib Puppet Playhouse (see page 86), for exceptional weekend puppet shows in an intimate 100-seat theater.

COOL KID'S CORNER: You won't believe this, but the floor of the Olympic-size pool here is hydraulic, meaning it can move up and down. In a matter of minutes, one end can go from six-feet deep to a shallow three feet. It can even be raised to zero feet. Imagine if you could do that in your bathtub—water would land all over the floor!

Books of Wonder

Address: 16 West 18th Street bet. Fifth and Sixth Avenues
Phone: 989-3270 • Ideal Age Group: 2 to 7
Admission: Free Sunday story readings at 11:45 A.M.

In his fascinating classic *The Read-Aloud Handbook*, Jim Trelease presents compelling evidence that the practice of reading to children is essential for awakening young imaginations, improving language skills, even bringing families closer together. He goes on to cite a 1983 National Academy of Education study that concluded, "The single most important activity for building the knowledge required for eventual success in reading is reading aloud to children."

The facts are irrefutable—a child who is read to regularly becomes a better reader, and good early readers go on to be enthusiastic students. There's even evidence that prenatal reading has a positive effect on an unborn child's learning abilities. Powerful stuff. All of which is overshadowed by the simple fact that reading aloud is fun for both adult and child.

My observation is that parents are reading to children like never before. But when you're simply maxed out on picture books or run low on reading steam, there's help available from a few excellent children's bookstores with regular story hours—some embellished with appearances by lovable storybook characters in costume.

For many years, one dedicated children's bookstore has been a reliable friend to kids who love stories, offering delightful weekly presentations in a clean, pleasant environment—Books of Wonder. The store's consistently friendly, animated readers have access to thousands of titles in this bright, colorful, carpeted store, so your children are always exposed to the best in classic and contemporary picture books.

Parents will also note that Books of Wonder has one of the largest selections of collectible children's books in the city, including all those we loved: The Hardy Boys, Nancy Drew, The Bobsy Twins, along with early editions of Frank Baum's *The Wonderful Wizard of Oz*.

If Books of Wonder's downtown location is inconvenient, here are some other Manhattan bookstores with regular readings: **Barnes & Noble Jr.** (120 East 86th Street between Park and Lexington Avenues/427-0686) and **The Bank Street Bookstore** (610 West 112th Street at Broadway/678-1654). Check with your local library, too. They may have a children's reading nook with a scheduled story hour each week.

COOL KID'S CORNER: Some of your favorite authors and illustrators come to Books of Wonder just to see you. Ask for a calendar of appearances by writers like Chris Van Allsburg *(The Polar Express, Jumanji)*, Eric Carle *(The Very Hungry Caterpillar)*, and Hillary Knight (illustrator for the Eloise stories).

Bronx Zoo
Wildlife Conservation Park

Address: Bronx River Parkway at Fordham Road, Bronx
Phone: 718-367-1010 • Ideal Age Group: 4 to 12
Admission: $6.75 adults/$3 children

Even if there were nothing here but the apes—celebrated twins, Ngomba and Tambo, and the rest of the gorilla gang scrambling for bananas and mugging for photos—this wonderful zoo would still be a surefire favorite, the no-brainer of unbeatable places to take children.

As it turns out, the largest urban zoo in the country has room for 4,000 other animals, all humanely kept in spectacularly designed natural habitats within the park's 265 acres. Which means that in one smartly planned visit, you and your children can go on an African safari to see tigers one hour and trek through the bat-infested jungles of Asia the next.

The famous Reptile House, where I got my first look at a steely-eyed crocodile as a kid, still has the kind of slithery attractions that children never forget—like Samantha, a twenty-two-foot python, and the largest snake on exhibit in the United States (with a torso twice the size of my thigh). If you're raising a young zoologist with a fondness for monkeys, walk over to JungleWorld, a rainforestlike setting that's home to playful gibbons, as well as a pair of intense black panthers.

And pray your noggin doesn't look like a ripe mango, because broad-winged fruit bats dart just inches above your head.

The Bengali Express, a guided monorail tour that passes over Wild Asia, offers a close-up look at an adorable rhino baby and rare sika deer. During a recent visit the line for this ride was very long, but once my friends and I were on the open-sided cars, close encounters with powerful elephants and regal Siberian tigers made the wait seem worthwhile.

If you're escorting children under seven, make tracks to the Children's Zoo (separate fee of $2 for adults; $1.50 for kids). This smaller enclosure within the wildlife center has short, mulch-lined walkways between exhibits that are gentler on a child's easily fatigued legs. The general theme at this zoo is "do as the animals do." So when I go, I make myself very small to squeeze through the prairie dog tunnels in a dirt mound adjacent to the real thing (fun, but best left to tinier bodies). Then I take the leap test to see if I can jump farther than a bullfrog (the bullfrog always wins), and I crawl inside one of three human-sized turtle shells, too. Finally, I like to stop by the petting zoo, buy a handful of food pellets that look like Grape Nuts, and let a brown llama tickle my palm with a soft muzzle. The adorable hip-high Shetland pony, however, invariably wins my heart.

COOL KID'S CORNER: Ever wonder what it would feel like to be a lizard escaping down a hollow tree? You can find out at the Children's Zoo where they've placed a slippery spiral slide inside a giant imitation oak. Just climb the stairs to the tree house and take the long ride down. After four topsy-turvy descents during my last visit, my girlfriend said we had to go. Darn, the other kids got to stay!

Central Park Wildlife Center

Address: Fifth Avenue at 64th Street • Phone: 861-6030
Ideal Age Group: 2 to 12
Admission: $2.50 adults/50¢ children

I had just picked my spot around the open-air pool to watch the 4 P.M. sea lion feeding. The sleek brown swimmers were doing that neck-craning thing they do—hoisting themselves up on the rim of their glass-enclosed sea, snorting a fine spray, trying to catch a glimpse of the fish-filled buckets coming their way. Nearby, an excited little boy with his nose pressed against the tank said to his friend, "Tommy, when you grow up do you want to work at the zoo?"

Putting aside any personal feelings you have about small urban zoos caging wild animals, you can appreciate just how magical the Central Park Wildlife Center must be to a four-year-old who would ask this question. To him, the zoo is so cool, so captivating, so much fun, he'd like to spend the rest of his life here. That's a major endorsement. Time to book the play date.

Even if you live in the city and have visited the wildlife center a hundred times, make it a hundred and one—there's always more for you and your kids to discover here. I never saw the tree-napping red pandas until my fourth trip, and I often find peculiar new critters in the Tropic Zone who were hiding on previous visits. Don't forget, too, that kids thrive on the repeat experience which gives them a sense of mastery over their environment, along with a security born of familiarity. I love to watch children confidently escorting smaller siblings along the richly landscaped paths to see the "ice bears" or the monkeys with the "red tushies." This zoo is particularly well-suited to tiny bodies with little feet, because they can meander easily through the entire compact habitat in a short time.

Stop in the Tropic Zone first where you'll find hundreds of monkeys (the white-maned tamarins will charm you), reptiles, and tropical birds, along with tanks of exotic fish (turns out piranhas really can strip the flesh off a city rat in seconds). This steamy, two-story natural jungle—an ideal antidote for cold winter days—also houses a humongous ant farm where children can watch thousands of leaf-cutter ants dart through deep catacombs via miniature closed-circuit cameras.

From here, children usually lead the way to favorite destinations like the polar bear exhibit where Gus, the internationally known brooder, has all but stopped his compulsive swimming laps. I also like the shivery Edge of the Ice Pack because I can't get enough of those zippy penguins shooting out of the water bolt upright onto the rocky shoreline.

COOL KID'S CORNER: Stop by the zoo's north gate below the Delacorte Clock. Every half hour the time is chimed while you watch the slow pirouettes of an elephant playing the accordion, a hippo on the violin, a mountain goat tooting a flute, a penguin beating a drum, a dancing bear with a tamborine, and a horn blowing Mama kangaroo with her baby. And, of course, there's the playful pair of monkeys on top thumping the bell!

Chelsea Piers Sports & Entertainment Complex

Address: Piers 59 to 62 at 23rd Street on the Hudson River
Phone: 336-6500 • Ideal Age Group: 2 to 12
Admission: Free to piers/Activities as low as
$2.50 for all-day roller rink access

This gigantic waterfront sports and recreation center was built on the kind of scale New Yorkers love—what I call "the only" scale: the only four-story, year-round golf driving range in the country, the only indoor ice-skating rinks in Manhattan (one each for hockey and figure skating), the only outdoor, professionally surfaced Roller-Blading rinks in Manhattan, and the only gymnastics training area in New York City sanctioned for competition by USA Gymnastics. And that doesn't even cover the largest and longest categories —largest rock climbing wall in the Northeast and longest indoor running track in the world, at a quarter mile.

Those of us familiar with the imposing size of skyscrapers might best comprehend the sheer mass of this complex (and by extension, all it has to offer kids) by thinking of four eighty-story buildings lying down. Stretched over historic shipping piers, all 1.7 million square feet are designed to deliver maximum high energy fun for sports-starved children and adults.

The central attraction for kids is the main Field House, with two indoor AstroTurf soccer fields, a twenty-eight-foot rock climbing wall specially designed for children, basketball courts, four batting cages ($1 for a dozen swings to hit it out), plus a massive gymnastics facility (in-ground trampoline, rings, pommel horses, balance beams, parallel bars, you name it). Be sure to take a plunge into the foam-filled diving pit, too, but hang onto your keys.

The Sky Rink was more or less the catalyst for Chelsea Piers. Developer Roland Betts was looking for a practice facility for his figure-skating daughter, Jessie, after the original Sky Rink closed on Thirty-third Street. Good father that he was, Betts got some friends together, borrowed $100 million, and erected this mega sports mall. Now Jessie and every other kid in New York City can turn figure eights twenty-two hours a day.

I've never been to an Olympic Sports Village, but it must be a lot like this—safe, sanitized, steeped in primary colors, with athletes of every age walking in leotards and Lycra, looking fit and healthy. The user-friendly Chelsea Piers is such a total sports resource, a number of area schools are abandoning their physical education programs and bussing their kids over here to have an absolute field day.

COOL KID'S CORNER: I don't know many kids who are golfers (on the other hand, Tiger Woods must have started young), but whether you own golf clubs or not, drag your duffer dad over to the four floors of ball-whacking wildness at the Chelsea Piers Golf Club. You won't believe your eyes when those little white balls are teed up for you automatically. They're retrieved from the 200-yard driving range by machine, too!

Children's Museum of the Arts

Address: 72 Spring Street bet. Lafayette and Broadway
Phone: 274-0986 • Ideal Age Group: 2 to 8
Admission: $4 per person weekdays/
$5 per person weekends

A small sign at the front desk of the Children's Museum of the Arts captures the child-friendly vibes that exude from this art studio and play space: *We request that you respect the needs of our young visitors, remembering that this is their special environment.*

Special indeed. At New York City's only children's museum that focuses solely on the arts, kids will find 5,000 square feet of art projects, performance space, and interactive exhibitions that submerge them in exuberant creation. If there is any question that this formula succeeds with toddlers and younger children, all you have to do is check out the stroller parking lot by the entrance, and the four-foot-high wooden shoe used to store countless pairs of Stride Rites and Weeboks.

Kids this young don't know much about art, but they know if you stick a few jars of tempera paints in front of them with permission to smear the colorful contents all over a tabletop, it's going to be a blast. The idea here is to encourage children to be expressive, independent, playful, and inquisitive as they experiment with artwork—all of which is adult code for anything goes. In fact, the informal motto here is *you can smell it, touch it, and play with it, just don't eat it.*

Besides exploring various messy mediums during daily art projects—including paint, pastels, collage, sand painting, origami, and more—children swarm to a fantastic play corral called the "Monet Ball Pond." Here, surrounded by a soothing Monet-inspired mural, girls and boys get bouncy, throwing their bodies with obvious pleasure into dozens of huge blue, green, orange, and red rubber balls. Museum founder Kathleen Schneider says this is an ideal way for children to work large muscles and blow off some steam before sitting down to a focused art project.

Other innovative exhibitions include a space where the floors, walls, and every surface in sight are painted with a blackboard substance for creating chalk art. Smaller children like to spend time in a skylit Colorforms area to explore line, shape, and color on a six-foot Plexiglass easel. A comfortable, carpeted roomlet called "Magnetic Masterpieces" is where reproductions of children's paintings have been cut into magnetic puzzles for assembly. You'll also find plenty of action at the two-story furnished playhouse and, finally, there's the magnificent Wonder Theatre where kids can make costumes and props and perform stories on stage in a safe, nonjudgmental environment.

COOL KID'S CORNER: If you love to sing-along and make loud, wonderful music with clangy pans, kooky kazoos, and cheechy maracas, then visit the indoor Music Garden at the museum every day (except Monday) at 12:30 P.M. and 4:30 P.M. The merry music man will make you smile.

Claremont Riding Academy

Address: 175 West 89th Street at Amsterdam Avenue
Phone: 724-5100 • Ideal Age Group: 6 to 12
Admission: $35 for 30-minute private lesson;
$35 for 1-hour group class

I wrote a children's video about youth rodeo once and got a chance to see lots of kids on horseback competing in Pennsylvania. Here were boys and girls small enough to crawl inside Hoss's hat—some as young as five—skillfully riding spirited, full-grown quarter horses. What impressed me most was the level of mastery and poise these children displayed with their mounts—a confidence, I imagined, that would help them in every aspect of their lives.

Lucky for city kids, there is an extraordinary place in the middle of New York City where young people can learn to handle horses with the proficiency of their country counterparts—Claremont Riding Academy. The century-old, five-story stable on 89th Street looks so startlingly out of place tucked into the urban density of the Upper West Side, a visit even for non-riding children should be placed on your must-do list.

If you have children older than six who've caught the riding bug, Claremont—with its fifteen professional riding instructors who respect kids and always stress safety awareness—is an ideal school for equestrian training. The academy offers reasonably priced private lessons (English saddle only) for beginners, as well as after-school and weekend group classes. They also have an acclaimed riding program for handicapped and special needs children (hanging out with horses, it seems, can be very therapeutic). In the summer, Claremont's popular day camp offers kids more concentrated instruction at a thirty-acre sister facility in nearby Leonia, New Jersey.

Built in 1892 (with few visible improvements since then) the landmark New York City stable is funky but fun, with the horsey essence of hay and manure filling a small ground floor riding arena that assures year-round classes. Claremont boards more than fifty horses here, from ponies and palominos to bays and grays, fully trained for all levels of riders. Whether your child saddles up on Bo-Peep, Caraway, Paddington, Drifter, Yosemite, or any of the other city-savvy horses, they'll learn good horsemanship and quickly conquer their fear of big animals. And when your kids become crackerjack horsemen, they can trot through Central Park on more than six miles of picturesque bridle paths.

COOL KID'S CORNER: Know what they have on the floors above the horse stalls? Really old carriages, buggies, and sleds from the days when people traveled the city by horse. And, hey (I know, hay is for horses), see if you can find the two horseshoes embedded in the sidewalk right out front of Claremont. Wonder if a dopey horse stepped in wet concrete a hundred years ago and lost his shoes?

Conservatory Garden

Address: 105th Street and Fifth Avenue
Phone: 860-1382 ● Ideal Age Group: 3 to 12
Admission: Free

There are 26,000 acres of parks and more than 860 playgrounds in New York City but only one formal garden—the spectacular Conservatory Garden on upper Fifth Avenue. Why, you ask, would my child be interested in six acres of precisely planted flower beds, arbor covered walkways, a perfectly manicured lawn, and two sculpted fountains, without a seesaw or slide in sight? Think fantasy, dear parent, think *The Secret Garden*.

Set off from the rest of Central Park by a mighty wrought iron fence and dropped below street level, the Conservatory Garden has a stately Victorian presence, a magical not-in-New-York quality that appeals to children. Little girls love to imagine they're stepping through the grounds of an English palace—what better place to play a princess in the court of kings? This has also become a popular destination for bride watching (wedding parties are here every weekend in the spring and summer, using the garden as a bucolic backdrop for photographs), where young misses can pick up style tips for dressing wedding bell Barbie.

The carefree safety of the garden also encourages city

boys to be more like country boys, darting through countless hidden niches and winding paths, all ideal for a pretend skirmish in Sherwood Forest or a more contemporary game of hide-and-seek with parents and siblings.

Another unusual offering of the Conservatory Garden is a place to sit quietly with your child, flanked by crab apple trees swaying to gentle breezes. The air always seems to be filled with birdsong here, and three seasons of the year it's heavy with the scent of fragrant flowers, too. Make no mistake, kids are powerfully effected by the beauty of nature. Carry a good storybook into this pristine setting on a spring day (when thousands of multicolored tulips are in bloom), set yourself down with your favorite four-year-old on a sweet and shady bench, and you'll make a lasting impression on a young soul.

The Urban Park Rangers (1-800-201-PARK) offer an active schedule of outdoor workshops, guided walks, and activities for kids conducted throughout our city parks. Give them a call and get on their mailing list. Also note the close proximity of the Dana Discovery Center (see page 117) just five blocks north, where they have exceptional nature programs for children throughout the year.

COOL KID'S CORNER: If you've read Frances Hodgson Burnett's _The Secret Garden_, go quickly to the south end fountain, where a bronze Mary and Dickon are playing mischievously. I also heard some children say they saw elves and fairies stepping on the fountain's lily pads. Oh, look, there they are!

Dieu Donné Papermill

Address: 433 Broome Street bet. Crosby and Broadway
Phone: 226-0573 • Ideal Age Group: 6 to 12
Admission: Free tour/$150 for 2-hour papermaking
workshop for groups of up to 15

When Sesame Street was looking for just the right location to shoot an exciting, educational segment on the art of hand papermaking, they went to the Dieu Donné Papermill in lower Manhattan. Nobody knows how to turn pulp into paper or demonstrate this intriguing art to children better than the friendly folks at New York City's first full-scale hand papermill.

What is it about papermaking that keeps kids fully engrossed until the moment their colorful sheets are pulled from the water press? I think the answer's obvious—papermaking is wet and messy and fun.

It's also an amazingly simple process, and holding your first completed sheet of paper is a thrilling accomplishment no matter how old you are. That's what I discovered when I attended a hands-on workshop at Dieu Donné with an eager class of second graders. First, we got to see how the mill's skilled artists make the raw material for paper by cutting, shreading, and beating small pieces of cotton and linen in water to form a soupy, cellulose pulp.

Next, this macerated mash was poured into a big vat.

That's when the anticipation really swelled as my seven-year-old papermaking buddies and I realized we were going to get to play in this goop. Using basic tools—a mould (wooden frame covered with screen upon which paper is formed), a deckle (another frame that fits onto the mould to shape the paper sheet), and a felt (a woolen cloth upon which newly formed paper is pressed)—we all dipped into the pulp vat and began to shake out and form our sheets.

Then we threw in all sorts of squirtable pulp colors, collage materials, glitter, even leaves and flowers, to decorate our paper sheets. I made a small blue sheet with the initials A.I. squirted on top in yellow, which I thought was pretty cool. Until I looked over and saw that the blonde kid next to me had taken a wad of semidried pulp and squeezed it into a kind of paper baseball. Wish I'd thought of that.

There are a few ways to experience Dieu Donné: a free twenty-minute Mill Tour allows children to see the equipment used to turn rags into pulp and finished paper; a one-hour tour and talk offers a detailed look into the papermaking process and costs $75 for groups up to twenty-five; a two-hour, hands-on demonstration gives kids a chance to create their own paper sheets at a cost of $150 for up to fifteen kids (a unique birthday party idea).

COOL KID'S CORNER: After visiting Dieu Donné you'll be ready to make paper at home using your old blue jeans and rags (a great way to recycle). All you'll need is a household blender for beating pulp material, some water, and a simple frame and deckle. Hey, look, you're making paper!

Empire State Building
Observatory

Address: 34th Street and Fifth Avenue • Phone: 736-3100
Ideal Age Group: 5 to 12 • Admission: $4.50 adults/$2.25
children for observatory; $11.50 adults/$7.25 children for
observatory and Transporter Ride combo ticket

C lass trip, fifth grade, eighty-sixth floor of the Empire State
Building. A couple of friends and I were peering over the
edge of the outdoor observation deck, pressing our luck with
a uniformed guard standing nearby. Eventually he made us
step back, then, as if to stress the awesome destructive power
of a building this large, he proceeded to share a fascinating bit
of trivia that has stuck in my brain for thirty years: "You know,
if you dropped a penny from up here it would imbed itself five
inches deep in the sidewalk."

Cool! Of course, I had no idea at the time if this worth-
less factoid was true. But it flamed the formidable mystique of
the world's most famous building, and prompted me to buy
one of those cheap, five-inch scale models of the quarter-mile-
high skyscraper. That prized momento sat on my desk next to
a small bronze replica of the Liberty Bell (Philadelphia class
trip, eighth grade) until I left for college.

This city is blessed with another sky-high wonder of the
world—the Twin Towers of the World Trade Center. But I

think kids get a bigger Big Apple kick from the original sky-scraper—the famous pencil point where King Kong swatted down rickety biplanes and Tom Hanks got the girl in *Sleepless in Seattle* (sure, I've seen *An Affair to Remember*, but what kid remembers?). I also prefer the Empire State Building's central location in midtown where children get more visual bang for the buck, picking out notable sights at every compass point and identifying the five states visible from here—let me see, New Jersey, Pennsylvania, Connecticut, Massachusetts and, uhhh, New York.

Kids also enjoy the offbeat adventure of simply reaching the observatory. There are seventy-three elevators in this building, but for some strange reason not one of them goes directly to the eighty-sixth floor. You have to take one car to the eightieth floor, trek through office hallways to another shaft, then finish the trip up in a second elevator—all of which seems to punctuate the building's massive size.

Here's a travel tip: this is one of the world's most popular tourist attractions. Show up at the wrong time and the lines will overwhelm you. I suggest an early arrival at 9:30 A.M. or visit at dinner hour, between 5 P.M. and 8 P.M.

COOL KID'S CORNER: Ask your parents nicely (please, pretty please) to purchase a combination ticket for Dino Island at the TRANSPORTER RIDE (Concourse Level, 947-4299). Then, sit down, strap in, and hang on for a futuristic movie adventure in wild, computer-controlled seating. Synchronized to the on-screen action, your seat sways, rolls, bounces, and dives as you hunt dinosaurs with thrilling realism. In fact, if the ride hadn't been so short—only seven minutes—I would have included it as a top fifty destination.

Engine Co. #18

Address: 132 West 10th Street at Greenwich Avenue
Phone: 570-4218 • Ideal Age Group: 2 to 8
Admission: Free

Here's one of the great, little-known secrets about New York—its firehouses are for kids. There's one in your neighborhood, and inside it are these rolling red monsters ("Look, Mommy, a fire truck!") with awesome tires the height of third graders and water hoses as thick as giant boa constrictors. The firehouse is filled with real firemen and firewomen, too, and they all seem to have this universal characteristic—they like kids. The best part is, you can take your children to virtually any firehouse in the city and if they aren't blasting off to douse a blaze, you're invited to drop in for a firehouse fantasy tour.

Engine Co. #18 is a particular favorite of the young children in Greenwich Village because of one outstanding feature—the super-duper garage door. Like most engine companies in the city, the garage door at #18 was decoratively painted for a firehouse competition during the 1976 Bicentennial. When the bicentennial was over, and every other firehouse door in the city was repainted red, the local community wanted this festive garage door to remain as it was for the celebration and so agreed to pay for its upkeep. Now the determined image of Uncle Sam at the wheel of engine #18, with two firemen at his side and a trusty dalmation riding shotgun, is yours to see anytime.

Inside, Captain Jim Gerrish and his twenty-five firefighters spend their day on one of three floors of this original brick firehouse, built in 1891. There's lots of hospitality here—just ask and your child will be hoisted into the front cab of the Mack pumper. Or get a bumper-to-bumper tour of the big rig with all its gauges and gadgets. You can also see the tiny House Watch booth where they throw the alarm to summon the firefighters (ten to fifteen times a day), who rush down one of four brass slide poles to the waiting fire truck. Know why that spiral staircase is the only way to reach the upper floors? Because when fire wagons were pulled by horses, the horses had a bad habit of climbing straight stairs to hang out with the firefighters, making it nearly impossible to get them down. Spiral stairs did the trick.

If you've got a die-hard junior firefighter in the family, you might also consider a visit to the **New York Fire Museum** (278 Spring Street/691-1303). Situated in a pristine former firchouse, this turn-of-the-century building is filled with Colonial leather fire buckets, torchlights, axes, alarm boxes, hose nozzles, and a fascinating, although slightly macabre, stuffed firehouse dog that was a favorite of his engine company in the 1940s.

COOL KID'S CORNER: Most of the firefighters you'll see leave their shoes untied or wear slip-on shoes. That's so they can kick them off fast when the alarm sounds and jump into a pair of those big boots and insulated pants lined up against the wall. You know, Engine Co. #18 was so much fun, I decided I want to be a fireman when I grow up.

FAO Schwarz

Address: 767 Fifth Avenue at 58th Street
Phone: 644-9400 • Ideal Age Group: 2 to 12
Admission: Free

There is probably no single name in New York more strongly associated with children than FAO Schwarz. This world famous toy store has been catering to the fantasies and imaginations of kids since 1862. At holiday time more than 50,000 eager children pull equally enchanted parents through the revolving doors of the Fifth Avenue store every day—a tradition that has continued for generations.

I said hello to the real-life toy soldier who greeted me at the front door on a recent visit, then became hypnotized by the endless spinning, flashing, bobbing, and bouncing of the animated Clock Tower. If you never took a step past the rolling blue eyes and chattering red lips of this famous singing timepiece—with its four tiers of chugging trains, blubbery blimps, and teetering toys—you could still keep a three-year-old fully engaged for fifteen minutes (try that with anything less than ice cream).

Of course, there are aisles and aisles of wonderful distractions delightfully displayed everywhere you look. When Frederick August Otto Schwarz stocked his shelves with simple European dolls and stuffed bears more than 130 years ago, he couldn't have guessed at the magnificent playroom his employees would create a century later in the world's largest toy store (okay, maybe there's a bigger Toys "Я" Us somewhere, but no toy store reigns larger in the minds of kids, and none treats children better).

This place is rocking. There are radio-controlled Formula One racers zipping past your feet, Barbie dolls smiling up at you, GI Joes circling around behind you. Star Wars figures invade this toyland, with wind-up toys squirming in every bin. There are more board games, movie-related action figures, and video games than all the fourth graders on earth could play with in a year. Electronic and science toys fill one blinking, buzzing display, while another area is stocked floor to ceiling with stuffed animals, including Truffles the Bear and Patrick the Pup—FAO's lovable mascots. And then there are more Barbies!

I got lost in the lollipop forest at the FAO Schweetz candy area where you'll see the Gummy Bear totem pole, the twelve-foot chocolate soldier, and the world's largest M&M's selection. One last thing: be sure to catch a ride on the giant robot elevator—"Go-to-Floor-Two"—with the red-tinted front window that always makes the busy street scene outside look rosey.

COOL KID'S CORNER: Here's why FAO Schwarz is the coolest toy store in the world—*they let any kid play with any toy in the store.* That means you can hug the teddy bears, swing the light sabers, twist the Gumby's, hop on a pogo stick, or play with the puzzles, and you won't get in a lick of trouble. That's the store rule. So say "ho" for FAO.

Forbes Magazine Galleries

**Address: 62 Fifth Avenue at 12th Street • Phone: 206-5548
Ideal Age Group: 5 to 12 • Admission: Free**

Nietzsche said it, but he could very well have been writing about Malcolm Forbes: "In every real man a child is hidden who wants to play."

Forbes, the consummate capitalist and successful publisher, had a great sense of humor, a wonderful capacity to fill himself with life, an adventurous spirit (he loved ballooning), and a penchant for collecting—most notably, Harley-Davidson motorcycles. And if you visit the Forbes Magazine Galleries, you'll discover that he was also into toys.

When you've got pockets as deep as Forbes', you can shop the auctions for goodies at a frantic pace. (Forbes said of his obsession for toy collecting, "Up went my hand, and it's not been often or long lowered since.") In fact, before he left this earthly playground, he'd gathered up 500 rare toy boats and 100,000 toy soldiers—not to mention a number of other priceless items like presidential letters, Abe Lincoln's stovepipe hat, inventor Charles Darrow's original hand-painted-Monopoly game board, and twelve of the ornate Faberge Easter Eggs made for the last czars of Russia. And they're all here to see.

Of course, it's the toys that draw kids from all over the world to this mazelike museum space. For young children accustomed to today's touch-it-all museum experience, the dignified Forbes Gallery might prove a bit frustrating—all these toy soldiers and no backyard to play in. But the elaborate scenes behind the display windows are so meticulously presented, the sheer numbers of rusting warships and tiny tin cowboys so striking, children leave deliciously lost in their imaginations.

None of the antique toys on display here were actual playthings from Forbes' early years, but he was able to snap up some amazing toys as a grown-up, including the only Lusitania model manufactured by famous toy ship builder Marklin. The doomed ocean liner lists precariously on the floor of a glass-bottomed sea with dozens of submarines hovering above, the telltale pinging of depth soundings filling the air (nautical music and blasts from throaty boat horns complete the mood in all the model boat galleries).

In the rooms dedicated to toy soldiers, someone has spent a very long time setting up marching scenes and mock battles between 12,000 of the more than 100,000 Civil War soldiers, medieval knights, Plains Indians, GIs, and Aztecs contained in the total Forbes' collection. My only gripe is that several of the display windows are too high for tiny eyes— look for one of the footstools scattered nearby.

COOL KID'S CORNER: "When I was sick and lay abed, I had two pillows at my head, and all my toys beside me lay, to keep me happy all the day." Just place your face in the circular window of Robert Louis Stevenson's *Land of Counterpane* and travel to his magical bedroom playland. You'll see.

Hippo Park Playground

Address: Riverside Park at 91st Street
Ideal Age Group: 2 to 7 • Admission: Free

Near the library of the small North Jersey town where I grew up, we had a thumb-sized park with a big green concrete frog poised to leap out the front entrance. He was such a sweet frog, so agreeable when hundreds of drooling toddlers climbed on his head and slid down his back, that the playground was fondly and forever christened Froggie Park.

It is with this same nostalgic fondness that I imagine every child who has ever played at Hippo Park will remember this friendly neighborhood playground when they've grown too big for happy hippos. Why hippos? Nobody knows. Maybe because it's a funny name kids love to say. In any case, there they are—seven adult hippos and six baby hippos, all frozen in various stages of wading and wallowing, some bellowing, others belching a spray fountain of water.

Even watching the park's smallest visitors, it's clear that hippos are happening. I saw an eighteen-month-old face-off with a big bull, shout some unintelligible demands at him with broad gestures, slap him on his broad snout, then march away. Like my Froggie, he was tolerant to the end.

One unusual aspect of this very safe park is that it's cooperatively maintained by the Parks Department and an all-volunteer community group called The Playground Project. Consisting primarily of local parents, this hardworking group raises funds for the upkeep and improvements in the park, employment of a full-time playground attendant year-round (when's the last time you saw that?), and installation of Riverside Park's first yellow emergency phone.

Besides the hippopotami, the oval-shaped, intimate playground is ideally designed for kids under seven, with four seesaws, three Sutcliffe swings for toddlers, plenty of conventional swings, two sandboxes (the clean, asbestos-free sand is replaced three times a year), wooden climbing gyms, and four slides including a neat spiral model—all shaded by magnificent fifty-year-old oaks.

Now here is every child's favorite thing to do at the Hippo Park: go to the center cluster of adult hippos, and scream as loud as you want into the big bull's cavernous mouth. Smaller kids can finish off by climbing down his throat and sliding out his belly.

COOL KID'S CORNER: For special fun, run to the big boulder at the south end of the playground. Now look closely and see if you can find the little animals clinging to the rock—three bronze turtles, three frogs, two snakes, the rat eating a snake, a bird, and a tiny mouse. They may be hiding, but they're all there—I promise.

Homboms

Address: 1500 First Avenue at 78th Street
Phone: 717-5300 • Ideal Age Group: 2 to 10
Admission: $7.95 to $15.95 for materials on most projects

T he scene: a rainy summer Saturday, your five-year-old has just watched *101 Dalmatians* for the second time and looks to be rewinding for a third viewing, while your seven-year-old is having a fit, kicking the kitchen cabinets out of frustration and boredom. The challenge: find something to do, Mom, quick!

There's lots to do at Homboms (formerly Crafts on Broadway), where they specialize in walk-in crafts for kids. Not only is this a palace for plastercraft painting—with more than 150 different molds lining the walls, from unicorns and turtles to dinosaurs and bulldogs—but children can also try their hands at sand art, fabric decorating on T-shirts, stationery making, trinket and treasure box painting, and more. Each project price is based on the size of the piece your child selects, and then little artists have as much time as they need to complete their masterpieces.

The folks at Homboms try not to interfere with the creative process, letting children layer on nontoxic base coat and colorful top coat paints to their hearts content. Owner Barbara Goldfarb's philosophy is that over-instruction and touch-ups are no-no's. She says it's more gratifying for a child to paint to their best ability—however inventive the final product might be—than to perfect the originality out of pieces. Attendants are standing by to assist if more sand lands on the workshop table than the peel-and-paint surface, or a wet plaster dolphin ends up in a lap (old men's shirt smocks are provided free).

Ask about Homboms' extensive crafts class schedule with offerings like origami paper sculpture, puppet making, mask painting, and collage. You should also note that Homboms can draw a daunting crowd of kids on rainy or wintry weekends—so plan to arrive early or late in the day.

P.S. The precast plaster experience is repeated at the **Little Shop of Plaster** (106 West 90th Street/877-9771) in a relaxed, pleasant storefront space. The college-age employee assigned to set up the paint stations on a recent visit was very good-natured and attentive, encouraging a pair of sisters to add a tenth color to their already psychedelic cats. Simple sand art and plastercraft projects start at $3.95. I liked the sign they had hanging on the wall, presumably not intended for the younger clientele: *If a cigarette urge is in your head, how about a piece of plastercraft instead?*

COOL KID'S CORNER: If you love crafts like bead stringing, modeling with clay, working with stamps and ink pads, playing with stickers, or creating interesting costumes decorated with acrylic stones and jewels, then Homboms is a great place to buy your arts and crafts projects to take home. Who knows, maybe someday I'll see your Sculpey clay jewelry on sale at the flea market.

Intrepid Sea-Air-Space Museum

Address: Pier 86 at West 46th Street on the Hudson River
Phone: 245-0072 ● Ideal Age Group: 5 to 12
Admission: $10 adults/$5 children

Remember the song, "War, what is it good for, absolutely nothing, listen to me. . . ." No, listen to me. The Intrepid, a World War II aircraft carrier loaded with hundreds of decommissioned military airplanes and artifacts is good fun for the whole family.

The imposing flattop is part of the world's largest naval museum—a truly amazing sight with a flotilla of six mothballed ships permanently parked in the New York harbor. This moored monument to America's military might changes all the time, too, with guest ships docking nearby frequently, and the U.S. Navy helicopter carrier *Guadalcanal* scheduled to open in 1997.

The Intrepid, with a long history of activity in World War II and Vietnam and as an astronaut recovery vessel, is the crown jewel of the fleet. In the cavernous interior hangars, three football fields long, you can watch some gripping war footage at the Carrier Operations Theatre (but with no seats, kids get antsy), walk in the shadow of stubby-nosed Grumman fighters, and shoehorn your body into the cockpit of an actual fighter jet.

The hangar and flight decks are stocked with what seems to be every retired military plane and spacecraft the museum could get its hands on (more than seventy)—and some look like they were rescued moments before hitting the junk heap. But children rarely notice the disrepair or the rust; just keep them moving because there's lots to see.

One of the few places young history buffs can actually talk to a World War II veteran is up on the ship's command bridge, where they've stationed a former sailor loaded with lots of Intrepid trivia. I heard wonderful tales from a weather-beaten seaman with an authentic forearm tattoo. And when he's done sharing war stories, this patriot polishes a gaggle of bronze instruments to a glossy spit shine.

You've got your choice of a destroyer (the *Edson*), a missile submarine (the *Growler*), an escort ship (the *Slater*), a lightship (the *Nantucket*), or a research vessel (the *Fisher*) to see next. My choice would be the USS *Growler*. In this former nuke-carrying sub, children can see the tight quarters where submerged sailors lived for weeks at a time. High points of this guided claustrophobia tour include the stainless steel showers (smaller than a Manhattan studio apartment's), sleeping quarters squeezed alongside the missile bays, and hatch doorways you'll definitely conk your head on unless you're under ten and very nimble.

COOL KID'S CORNER: If you were impressed with the alien spaceships in *Independence Day*, wait until you see the Lockheed A-12 Blackbird—our planet's highest-flying, fastest aircraft. This coal-black monster is a deadly sky streaker that flies at Mach 3—triple the speed of sound!

Island Helicopter

Address: Heliport at 34th Street on the East River
Phone: 683-4575 • Ideal Age Group: 5 to 12
Admission: Varying tours from $49 to $134 per person

When I was seven years old, my mother took my sister and me on a helicopter tour from the top of the old Pan Am building in midtown. It made such an impression, I can close my eyes today and still feel the lurching liftoff of my first helicopter ride.

There are several helicopter sight-seeing services in Manhattan, but the largest and most experienced organization (twenty-five years), with the best tours for the money, is Island Helicopter flying out of the Thirty-fourth Street Heliport. I also found that their handsome red, white, and blue fleet included the safest state-of-the-art aircraft—important when your family is aboard.

Island is open year-round from 9 A.M. to 9 P.M. (except Christmas Day), so your kids can get a bird's-eye view of the dazzling skyscrapers anytime of day, in any season (no reservations required). The skyline by night seems to appeal to adults more than kids, so pick a sunny, windless day for your trip. And arrive early so your children can spend some time at the heliport's big windows watching the constant stream of helicopters glide onto the tarmac. You can also go outside, walk south around the trailer office, and stand along the storm fence feeling the propellers buffeting the air as the whirlybirds make their vertical ascents.

I recommend Flight Package #2 ($64 per person) which covers fourteen miles from the United Nations to the Statue of Liberty, or about twenty minutes of airtime from takeoff to touchdown. If that sounds quick, consider that every minute is chock-full of excitement and simply unforgettable. You'll climb above the East River and the Brooklyn Bridge, ascend to the height of the Twin Towers, then stare straight into the eyes of the Big Green Lady before you loop back to the heliport.

Okay, it's pricey. But if you want my advice, save the $300 you'd pay Cuddles the Clown for birthday party entertainment, and take your son or daughter with three best friends to Island Helicopter instead. You'll be awarded Parent of the Year.

COOL KID'S CORNER: If you're the birthday boy or girl, ask for the single seat in the cockpit next to the uniformed pilot. You'll get a close-up look as he maneuvers the aircraft with a gazillion buttons and switches, and you'll peer down through your legs out the copter's glass nose. You can really feel the G-forces of the banking curves when you're sitting up front, too. It's awesome!

Jeremy's Place

Address: 322 East 81st Street bet. First and Second Avenues
Phone: 628-1414 • Ideal Age Group: 3 to10
Admission: Free

Remember going down to the local five-and-dime store when you were a kid and buying an excellent toy with your allowance money that you'd play with nonstop for a week—a balsa wood glider with a rubber band engine and a red plastic propeller, or a Superball that you could bounce over the roof?

In a world of $200 Nintendo games and $100 skateboards, it's hard for a city kid to find total toy satisfaction for under a buck. Unless you take your child (along with a few of his or her best friends) to Jeremy's Place.

Jeremy Sage has been doing children's birthday parties for more than thirty years, and his Upper East Side storefront and party place has earned a reputation for putting on the neatest and silliest parties in town for children ages two to ten. But what's really cool about Jeremy's Place is the front room jam-packed with more than 180 different toys for kids, most priced from 11¢ to 88¢.

Kids go absolutely wild here sifting through the dozens of widemouthed plastic jars (all thoughtfully placed at a child's eye level) filled with squirting spiders, wandering eyeballs, wind-up dinosaurs, witches fingertips, giant scissors, rainbow viewers, invisible ink, and tiny animals that grow gigantic inside soda bottles. The most popular item in the store is an icky 9¢ rubber worm Jeremy buys from a Florida bait supplier. He pays the supplier to remove the hooks, then sells 20,000 of these multicolored night crawlers during Halloween alone.

Besides his Pip Squeak Corner with really big toys for little tikes, Jeremy's got the best Glow in the Dark cave in town, too. Loaded with glow jewelry, jiggly glow snakes, creepy spiderwebs, and all sorts of neon Slinkies, the cave has become the prime spot for picking party bag favors.

Jeremy prides himself on selling no guns, no horns, no pointy things, no mean-spirited jokes, and no whoopee cushions. Just lots of colorful, inexpensive toys that spin, rotate, and bounce—and all his stuff is child safe and swallow proof, too. I like Jeremy and Jeremy likes kids. So if you've got a dollar and a child, go to Jeremy's.

COOL KID'S CORNER: You'll get a kick out of Jeremy's newest, handmade creations—Funny Foods. This humorous collection of amazingly true-to-life foods spills (coffee on a floppy disk, melted ice cream on the furniture) are sure to freak out your Mom or get a startled reaction from teachers. But watch your family dog—he may be so fooled by Funny Foods, he'll try to gobble up the freeze-dried mess.

Jodi's Gym

Address: 244 East 84th Street bet. Second and Third Avenues
Phone: 772-7633 • Ideal Age Group: 2 to 12
Admission: Starts at $410 for 17-week class/
$24 for 1-hour class

The gold medal performance of our women's gymnastic team in the 1996 Atlanta Olympics created a boon for many kid's gyms in the city. Suddenly, children who'd never executed a somersault were dreaming of perfect back flips, and parents were signing up aspiring gymnasts for after-school classes.

When this surge of fitness interest dies down, one heralded gymnastics studio will be training kids exactly the way they've been doing it in New York for fifteen years—Jodi's Gym. Jodi Rosenwasser-Levine, a former competitive gymnast, may well be the innovator of the tumbling tots phenomenon, and if the popularity of her classes are any indication, the offerings here are arguably the best.

While Jodi's Gym has a number of excellent preschool movement classes for the tiniest tumblers, this is not a drop-in play space. It's a bona fide gymnastics training facility with a staff of teachers certified by the U.S. Gymnastics Federation. A number of Jodi's students have even advanced to compete on a national level. And although Jodi stresses that maximum results in strength, flexibility, coordination, and balance are achieved over time, it is possible for out-of-town visitors to arrange for a short series of classes or even single visits (apparently, the children of actors, celebrities, and foreign dignitaries frequent this Upper East Side location and Jodi accommodates their erratic schedules). So if you're a tourist with restless kids who have had enough sightseeing and want exercise, consider Jodi's.

The focus here is always on fun, and the creative classes for kids under five are filled with delighted shrieks and giggles as children jump and shake, twist and tumble, reach, rattle and roll—all the body movements that are basic to gymnastics. Even the youngest kids are exposed to simple, well-padded apparatus like slides, doughnut mats, rings, bars, balance beams, balls, and bouncers.

There seem to be two important keys to the longevity of Jodi's Gym. First, talented teachers who like to be with kids. Jodi boasts a student-teacher ratio of six-to-one, but in a class of four-year-olds I observed there were actually nine kids to three staffers. I was impressed with the senior instructor who told stories to engage his class while stretching, like the one about the spider walking down the leg to catch the toes (not one kid spaced out during this entire exercise). The other factor is safety. Jodi's Gym is known as one of the safest gyms in the country, with a negligible accident rate. Good news when your daughter's doing her first cartwheel dismount off the balance beam.

COOL KID'S CORNER: If you're into cool leotards, leggings, skatetards, and sweatshirts, you'll find a fully stocked active wear store for boys and girls on the first floor.

Kerbs Conservatory Water Sailboats

Address: Central Park at 72nd Street near Fifth Avenue
Phone: 673-1102 • Ideal Age Group: 4 to 12
Admission: Sailboat rental $10 per hour

It has an old-fashioned, almost Victorian feeling about it that is leisurely and agreeable. Sailing a model boat with a young mariner is the kind of activity perfectly paced for an early spring morning or late summer afternoon. And at the Conservatory Water, they even supply the radio-controlled model yachts.

The oval-shaped boat pond sits in a small valley originally intended to be a formal garden with a glass conservatory. But park designers, Frederick Law Olmstead and Calvert Vaux, ran out of money, so the two-acre basin became a venue for ice-skating and model boat races. In 1929, the pond was rimmed with the low concrete wall you see today, so children can lean over and push their boats into the shallow waters.

If you own a model sailboat, you can use the Conservatory Water for sailing from the middle of March through November. Rental boats are available from early May through the end of October—look for the pushcart concession located at the halfway point of the east side footpath. Generally, two boats are recommended, one for parent and one for child, so you can stage your own informal races.

These model boats have no motors, and the radio controls only move the rudders and sails. Still, with the simple handheld control box, even young children can master operation of these miniyachts in minutes. The rental boats, with sails no higher than eighteen inches, can also be effective for teaching the basic concepts of sailing to those who've never ventured out on a full-sized Sunfish. Somehow, it's a lot easier to practice tacking maneuvers when you're not worried about getting clocked by the mainsail or tossed overboard.

Parents should note that the Hans Christian Andersen storybook statue on the west side of the Conservatory Water is home to a wonderful summer tradition—Saturday morning storytelling at 11 A.M. Children will hear myths, fairy tales, and legends from around the world, including engaging stories by the renowned creator of this park program, Diane Wolkstein.

COOL KID'S CORNER: If you want to see some really spectacular model boats with polished wooden hulls and sails as tall as you are, take a peak inside Kerbs Memorial Boathouse (at the Fifth Avenue side of the pond next to the food stand). That's where the privately-owned yachts are stored, many ranging in price from $500 to $1200. These prized boats are raced by serious sportsmen during the summer months; Saturdays at 10 A.M.

Kerlin Learning Center
at Wave Hill

Address: West 249th Street and Independence Avenue, Riverdale, Bronx • Phone: 718-549-3200 • Ideal Age Group: 2 to 8 • Admission: $4 adults/Free for children under 6/Free for everyone from November 15–March 15

Every Saturday and Sunday, fifty weeks a year, the Family Art Project at Wave Hill gives city kids a chance to smell, feel, touch, even taste an unspoiled bit of nature. As they explore the beautiful gardens, spacious lawns, and peaceful wooded trails of this spectacular twenty-eight-acre oasis, children learn about nature by being in nature—a positive, full-immersion experience that brownstone babies just can't get at the local dog run.

When I wrote *New York's 50 Best Places to Find Peace and Quiet*, I included Wave Hill as a spectacular retreat for nature-deprived city folk. I remember thinking then how valuable all this open space would be for overcrowded city kids. And that was before I knew about their creative programs to connect children to the natural world.

On weekend afternoons from 1 P.M. to 4 P.M., your children are placed in the capable hands of visual artist and naturalist, Noah Baen. Since 1990, Noah has guided kids through Wave Hill's lush landscape pointing out the shapes of leaves, the fragrances of flowers, the buzzing and fluttering of bees, butterflies, and birds. In the winter, when nature seems to sleep, Noah cleverly rolls back a big rock to see what crawls out or finds life on the end of a tree branch where none seemed to exist a moment before.

Then, the kids collect stuff: pinecones, seed pods, dry grasses, flower petals, chipped rocks, twisted gourds, variegated leaves, and all sorts of other wondrous outdoor bounty. Which, under Noah's watchful eye, is creatively transformed by the children into art: floral collages, ornamental wreaths, natural noisemakers, three-dimensional paintings, traditional corn husk dolls, and harvest headdresses. Much of this inspiring work can be found festooning the walls and hanging from the ceiling of the Kerlin Learning Center, located in the basement of Wave Hill's main facility—a spectacular stone mansion built in 1843.

Noah is a superb teacher and respectful friend to the children who drop in for his inspiring, sensory workshops. He's not afraid to wear a butterfly wing hat to enhance a story about monarch migration, or a leaf mask to explain the miracle of fall foliage. Best of all, he enthusiastically admires every creation made here and offers each child his focused attention. Now there's a precious gift.

COOL KID'S CORNER: The neatest thing in the Kerlin Center is the active honeybee hive. Stick your ear against the glass hive walls to hear the low hum of buzzing bees, look for the queen with the white spot on her back, or inhale the sweet honey smell by putting your nose near the end vents. If you show up at harvest time you can even taste the yummy honey right off the waxy comb.

Liberty Science Center

**Address: 251 Phillip Street, Liberty State Park,
Jersey City, New Jersey • Phone: 201-200-1000
Ideal Age Group: 5 to 12 • Admission: $13.50 adults
w/OmniMax Theater/$9.50 children w/OmniMax Theater**

There's no escaping it, when I was young, science stunk. Biology, physics, chemistry, it didn't matter, they all left me sleepy and confused. Recess, on the other hand, was fun. I was totally focused during recess. Which leads me to the conclusion that if you could keep recess going while learning science, you'd have a winning formula.

Fortunately, they've figured all that out at the Liberty Science Center (LSC) where their motto is Science = Fun, and where they've packed a hulking steel-and-concrete structure with four floors of unforgettable scientific attractions. The moment I entered the front atrium to see the herky-jerky motions of the mesmerizing Hoberman Sphere (a 700-pound aluminium snowflake that explodes robotically from 4.5 feet to 18 feet in seconds), I knew science would never be the same.

This cavernous space reminds me of a vertical pinball machine, with hundreds of high-scoring, hands-on exhibits forming the bumpers, and kids playing the part of the hyper-active balls. The energy at LSC is intense, and children can be quickly overstimulated—plan to go slow and not rush through in one visit.

That said, let me take you on a brief tour of my five favorite discoveries. First, there's the Torsional Wave, a seventy-foot spinal column of metal rods that ascends to the ceiling three stories up. A sharp tug on the handle convulses the instrument, and traveling waves can be timed to the top and back. Virtual Hoops is next; enter the minicourt, slip on a cyber glove, then challenge a team of hootin' and hollerin' computer-generated players as you drive for the virtual basket (I got stuffed five times).

On the second floor, I was fixated by the Air Cannon, a place to blast a tennis ball sky high using a bowling ball and a cushion of compressed air (it's hard to explain, just do it). A short distance away was the Bernoulli Bench, where I tossed a beach ball toward an invisible column of blowing air and watched it dance and float in magical suspension. And my favorite was the world's largest OmniMax Theater hiding under that huge silver-skinned dome at LSC. Spectacular movies are projected inside this overhead vault, filling your entire visual field with 180 degrees of dazzling and dramatic pictures. My senses were flying.

All this and I've yet to mention the four-inch-long hissing Madagascar Cockroaches (go ahead, pick them up), the solar telescope for spotting sun flares, and dozens of remarkable mindbenders and interactive puzzles.

COOL KID'S CORNER: Ready for something creepy? Crawl through the pitch-black, 100-foot maze of the Touch Tunnel, where you have to trust every sense but your eyes to get you through. I wriggled my way slowly along, sweating bullets. Fortunately, everybody gets out alive.

Madison Square Garden Tour

Address: Seventh Avenue bet. 31st and 33rd Streets
Phone: 465-5800 • Ideal Age Group: 5 to 12
Admission: $9 adults/$8 children

There's no sports fan like a New York sports fan, and they tend to raise little fanatics. If you've got one running around your house wearing a Knicks or Rangers jersey, he or she is going to flip over this one-hour, behind-the-scenes tour of arguably the world's most famous sports arena (actually, I saw two kids with Chicago Bulls uniforms on who looked totally into it, too).

Even before the tour starts, you're treated to a fascinating, time-lapse video (shot over 104 days) of the Madison Square Garden floor being converted for basketball, boxing, hockey, the circus, and a rock concert (and to think they stage rodeos in here, too). Then the real fan fun begins.

A hip, black-clad tour guide whisks you through a posh, season ticket-holders dining room where you view a short video history of the thirty-year-old Garden (built in 1968, it's New York City's fourth Garden sports complex). Then you're taken upstairs to one of the eighty-nine lavish skyboxes overlooking the arena, containing a dozen cushy seats, a kitchen, a bar, and closed-circuit TVs—all available for the current price of just $300,000 per year. These, not surprisingly, are generally owned by large corporations to entertain business guests.

The next stop is where kids go absolutely wild: they're taken directly inside the Rangers or Knicks locker room (which one depends on who has a game that night—you visit the other team's quarters). Here, young fans see the actual players' lockers, their game uniforms, and the tables where the players get taped before games. This is a great opportunity to take your photo with Messier's jersey or Ewing's giant basketball shoes.

One six-year-old on our tour got to slip his foot into the size seventeen sneaker of a New York Knick superstar. Later, a locker room attendant tossed the same ecstatic little boy an official NHL hockey puck—yes, he got to keep it. Then the tour ends as you descend the stairs of this historic 20,000 seat arena to sit on the Rangers and Knicks home bench, listening to amazing facts about the massive Garden scoreboard and the making of the hockey ice (twenty hours). Our tour guide, an enthusiastic and obsessed New York sports fan, finished up by challenging members of our group to a sports trivia quiz. I didn't get one answer right—the six year-old got ten.

COOL KID'S CORNER: Take the last tour of the day if you want to bump into one of your favorite Knicks or Rangers arriving before a game (the guide said it happens all the time). Also look for the mini–hockey rink woven into the rug of the Rangers locker room so coaches can diagram plays between periods, and the specially cut Knicks locker room door that's a whole foot taller than any other door in the hallway.

NBC Studio Tour

Address: 30 Rockefeller Plaza at 50th Street bet.
Fifth and Sixth Avenues
Phone: 664-4000 • Ideal Age Group: 7 to 12
Admission: $10 per person

Whenever my starstruck nieces and nephews visit me in the media capital of the world, the question they always ask is, "Will I see anyone famous?" Predictably, we end up spending half our time maximizing opportunities for celebrity sightings—recent strategies being a trip to the Ed Sullivan Theater during Letterman tapings or strolls through celebrity- dense neighborhoods like tony Madison Avenue.

But now I've discovered a midtown destination with a very high probability of celebrity contact (defined by my 11-year-old nephew as a handshake or high five)—the NBC Studio tour. This one-hour guided tour into the bowels of the National Broadcasting Company is fascinating and fun, especially for older kids held spellbound by the allure of TV.

The tour departs from NBC's Rockefeller Center lobby and it's there at the main elevators where so many spottings occur. Guests from shows like *Rosie O'Donnell, Late Night with Conan O'Brien,* and *Saturday Night Live,* as well as many local news personalities, pass through the same halls and ride the same elevators as guests on the tour. Even if your "biggest" sighting is Al Roker (the station's congenial weatherman), you've earned bragging rights back home.

Some of the tour highlights for children are participation in a mock radio show (for which kids are always chosen) underscoring NBC's origins in radio. I particularly liked the Slap and Crack paddle used during radio sports broadcasts to mimick the sound of a bat hitting a baseball. You'll also get a peek into the studios of the *Dateline* and *NFL Today* programs, as well as a visit to *Studio 8H*, the legendary home of *Saturday Night Live*. Finally, you're taken to a working studio where one member of the tour is selected to do an on-screen weather report using a chroma key device. I volunteered and forecast an August snowstorm for New York. Wrong.

After your tour, take the family to Huxley's Cafe in the lobby for more star gazing. The reasonably priced eatery is practically an adjunct of the NBC cafeteria and frequented by network celebs. Huxley's also has a special kids menu for under $6, and a glass full of crayons on every paper-covered table.

Oh, I almost forgot—I saw Tom Brokaw (no high five) and local anchorwoman, Sue Simmons, during our tour. I can't wait to tell my nephew.

COOL KID'S CORNER: Here are some fun facts—the NBC mascot is a peacock because the network was the nation's first to broadcast in color. And those three tones you hear during station identifications are the musical notes G, E, C—the initials for NBC's corporate parent, the General Electric Company.

New Jersey
Children's Museum

Address: 599 Industrial Avenue, Paramus, New Jersey
Phone: 201-262-5151 • Ideal Age Group: 2 to 8
Admission: $7 per person

L ittle kids spend a major part of their playtime pretending to be adults—doing important grown-up jobs, dressing up in big people's uniforms, mimicking the words and actions of parents. It was only a matter of time before someone realized that creating a place specifically made for play-acting and pretending would be a hit with kids.

Aha! Look no further than the New Jersey Children's Museum. I know what you're thinking—since when did Paramus become one of the five boroughs? Since I decided that if you can drive out to the suburban malls to shop, your kids can enjoy a fun-filled afternoon as a surgeon, a ballerina, a knight in armor, a fireman, a helicopter pilot, a newscaster, an astronaut, an archaeologist, a construction worker, a boat captain, a postal worker, a chef . . . whew, I'll run out of space before this 15,000 square foot paradise of pretending runs out of ersatz professions!

The museum's converted warehouse location doubles as an exciting learning environment and world of fantasy, where kids are encouraged to touch and try everything. Do you have an aspiring hard hat in the house? The museum has a genuine orange Tiger Excavator in a nifty area that includes building blocks, construction toys, and cutaways of the warehouse structure itself so children can identify I-beams and cinder blocks.

For future pilots, they've flown in an authentic Hughes 269 helicopter with its dome cockpit and dashboard dials still in place. Your daughter the doctor can play in a hospital room with a real examining table, working stethoscopes, surgical gowns, and X-rays hanging from a light box. One of the most popular destinations is a mock grocery store complete with stocked shelves, kid-sized metal pushcarts, and a check-out register (what is it about bagging groceries that's so entertaining?).

Of the more than forty permanent exhibits, my favorite was the fully functioning television station, WKIDS, where children can watch themselves doing the news on two state-of-the art TV monitors. Right behind that was an outstanding ten-foot tall Fantasy Castle with formidable turrets, a kids-only velvet throne room, and a great assortment of medieval costuming to stage a magical Renaissance Fair. In the voting booth, young Americans can cast their ballots for Chelsea Clinton, and over at the horse stable, rodeo kids can ride a trio of stuffed stallions.

What do you want to be when you grow up? The New Jersey Children's Museum is the place to find the answers.

COOL KID'S CORNER: Climb aboard the real, 1954 open-cab fire engine that's ready to roll. Turn on the red flashing lights, pull the yellow cord to clang the bell, and rush to a blaze in full fire gear. You drive, I'll pull the pumper hoses. Let's go!

Places to Take Children **65**

The New Victory Theater

Address: 209 West 42nd Street
bet. Seventh and Eighth Avenues
Phone: 382-4000 • Ideal Age Group: 6 to 12
Admission: Show tickets are $10 to $25

"Adults ought to plead with their kids to be taken along to The New Victory!" That's what Donald Lyons of the *Wall Street Journal* said about the reopening of the former Victory Theater—Manhattan's oldest active theater built by Oscar Hammerstein in 1900. This intimate, elegant, 500-seat jewel box has been lovingly restored and is now fully established as New York City's first performing arts theater for children and families.

Until recently, Forty-second Street was the last place on earth you'd want to bring your kids. A fashionable theater district at the turn of the century, it had deteriorated by the 1970s and 1980s into a seedy strip of X-rated movie houses and peep shops. But under the direction of an independent, nonprofit organization called The New 42nd Street, this historic block has been revitalized and refurbished, and The New Victory is its first crowning achievement.

In this ornate, double-balconied auditorium—decorated in deep reds and gold, with eight pairs of chubby cherubs dangling their feet from the rim of a splendid central dome—young people are treated to sixteen dazzling productions of innovative new shows and celebrated classics every season. And make no mistake—this is not frivolous kiddie theater, unsuitable for adults in tow. These are thoughtful, inspiring, sometimes gritty or amusing stage productions, professionally performed with astonishing sophistication. Suddenly, great theater has been made accessible to kids—in their very own playhouse.

The New Victory has assembled a magical mix of presentations, from the story of *Peter Pan* told in the fantastic Bunraku-style of puppetry to acclaimed movement performances by the David Parsons and Alvin Ailey dance companies. There have been emotional dramatic plays, rousing musicals, fabulous film festivals, and comedy acts, too, including the hilarious juggling and clowning of the Flying Karamazov Brothers—a favorite show that always leaves the audience in fits of contagious giggling. A complete, colorful program of the full season schedule is available by calling the New Victory.

If there is any doubt that this handsomely restored theater has thoughtfully considered the entertainment needs of children, I'd like to point out one important detail: the theater is pitched more sharply than any I've ever seen. Which means that it's very easy for little heads to see over grandma's big hair in front.

COOL KID'S CORNER: They rebuilt the Victory's grand exterior staircase so kids like you could race to the top before the show begins. Once inside, look closely at the end of each row of seats. See those carved bumble bees—they were put there long ago by a former Victory owner named David Belasco. Get it ... BEE-lasco.

New York's Aquarium for Wildlife Conservation

Address: West 8th Street and Surf Avenue,
Coney Island, Brooklyn
Phone: 718-265-3474 • Ideal Age Group: 5 to 12
Admission: $7.75 adults/$3.50 children

Sharks can smell prey a mile away, hear prey a half mile away, see prey fifty feet away, and taste prey as they chomp away! But at the New York Aquarium you can get almost close enough to these ferocious-looking, prehistoric predators to brush those fifteen rows of razor-sharp teeth.

Although the aquarium celebrated its 100th anniversary in 1996 (the oldest continually operating aquarium in the nation), this waterside home to sharks, stingrays, beluga whales, walruses, dolphins, and thousands of fish and marine mammals is no longer the uninspired tank farm I remember from school outings as a kid.

For one thing, they've got a new name—New York's Aquarium for Wildlife Conservation. They've also added a dramatic Sea Cliffs Exhibit—a 300-foot rocky re-creation of a Pacific coastal habitat for sea otters, penguins, seals, and blubbery walruses. And, now, you can even be splashed at a new 1,600-seat Aquatheater, featuring Sea World-type shows twice a day with the air-and-sea antics of bottlenose dolphins and barking sea lions. Maybe I'm an easy audience, but to me there are few things as exciting as a streaking dolphin flying through the air to pluck a herring from the outstretched lips of his trainer.

The Discovery Cove features a Touch Tank filled with live sea stars and horseshoe crabs, along with other hands-on marine exhibits. There's also the amazing Crash Cave where you can live out your fantasy of being a barnacle. Every thirty seconds a man-made wave explodes overhead as you experience the unbelievable force of shoreline surf while remaining dry and unscathed. Wow, hang on!

The Cove also houses a crowd pleaser called "Fish That Go Zap!" Here your children can compare their body's electrical charges to the 650 volts generated by a slithery electric eel. Ugly, ugly, ugly. But the hyperactive, amplified crackles and pops of the measuring devices are cool for kids.

While the aquarium's odd-looking family of beluga whales (including the world's first whales born in captivity) are a perennial favorite, it's hard not to dash off to the 90,000 gallon shark tank the moment you arrive. Standing with your nose inches away from the deadly teeth and beady eyes of circling behemoths like Big Bertha (a 400-pound, 10-foot sandtiger) throws you and the kids into a delirious state of exhilaration and fear.

COOL KID'S CORNER: Could you stand the freezing cold of ocean life? Can you hold your breath as long as a seal? You can answer these and other questions in the Sea Cliffs Exhibit. I held my breath for forty-five seconds (a seal can dive for twenty minutes), and the icy metal plate used to test skin for deep water cold tolerance made me shiver. I guess I'll stay a human.

New York Doll Hospital

Address: 787 Lexington Avenue bet. 61st and 62nd Streets
Phone: 838-7527 • Ideal Age Group: 5 to 12
Admission: Free

Only in New York. Actually, this dedicated doll hospital is the only one in the entire United States. If that isn't reason enough to take the kids, how do 100 upside-down porcelain heads grab you? Or an equal number of spare torsos hanging from the backroom rafters?

I'm going to tell you right upfront that the New York Doll Hospital is a mess. Arms here, assorted legs over there, a pile of wigs in the corner, boxes full of eyeballs in the back. You'll probably be offended by the chaos and clutter, but any child who's ever left his toys lying around is going to love this place.

The nearly 100-year-old doll hospital is not only an international institution, it's the last survivor of a fast dying art. It's also incredibly weird. But if you can overlook the monstrous muddle for a minute, you'll notice something. Broken, battered, and bruised dolls of every size, shape, and pedigree are admitted here—and that's because proprietor Irving Chais is probably the finest doll doctor in the world.

Irving's grandfather started the hospital around 1900, and it's been in the family ever since. Irving grew up restringing dislocated arms, repairing torn dresses, and regluing pulled out hair. Today, the world's most respected doll manufacturers send him their repairs, and private collectors from as far as South Africa and Australia trust only Irving to treat their valuable Shirley Temples. He still works six days a week saving the lives of treasured dolls, assisted by an equally dedicated doctor from Colombia, a dressmaker who's been with him for thirty five years, and his daughter who specializes in wig reconstruction.

While he's not doing much surgery anymore, Irving is constantly digging out original spare parts for the vinyl, rubber, tin, wood, plastic, porcelain, papier mâché, and clay dolls brought here for repair. Besides his encyclopedic knowledge of dolls (he can identify the maker and country of origin of any doll you shove at him in seconds), Irving is also a funny man with some practiced one-liners. He's fond of saying that the hospital has "never lost a patient," and that his medical malpractice costs are zero.

COOL KID'S CORNER: Irving, who likes to play the grumpy old man, really adores kids and will be thrilled to show you his kooky collection of body parts. Ask him to take you in back to see the 100,000 pairs of glass eyes and the big box of creepy doll teeth. You're gonna love this guy.

New York Hall of Science

**Address: 47-01 111th Street,
Flushing Meadows Corona Park, Queens
Phone: 718-699-0005 • Ideal Age Group: 5 to 12
Admission: $4.50 adults/$3 children**

The good news is they've packed so many gee-whiz thrills into the spellbinding exhibits at the Hall of Science, your kids will devour every soft scientific principle with glee. The bad news is, not a child on earth could happily transition to a school textbook after a day on this unforgettable field trip. Oh well, sound-bite science is fun.

There are more than 160 amazingly cool, interactive exhibits here that look nothing like the boring, brain-drain experiments of my youth. In fact, I liked this hands-on science museum so much, I couldn't keep my hands off. I went back three times.

The Hall of Science was originally built as a pavilion for the 1964 World's Fair and they still have some circa aerospace artifacts rusting outside. But don't let these relics fool you— there's cutting edge intrigue inside, with enough fascinating experiments to fill a few afternoons. Check out the Distorted Room where people go from midgets to megasize before your eyes. The Touch The Spring illusion blew me away—I kept calling strangers over to grab the coil that wasn't there. The

Antigravity Mirror was totally weird (look, I'm flying!), and if you're into microbes and fungi, you can hunt for the infinitesimal beasties under powerful video microscopes—who knew there was all this action in a drop of pond water?

And don't freak out if an experiment puzzles you. There's an incredibly helpful staff of groovy geeks on hand (not a pocket protector in sight) to demonstrate everything. Generally, activities are fast and easy to execute, so kids can try a lot in a little time. The Hall of Science is also less hectic and crowded than the Liberty Science Center (see page 58), especially if you arrive after school groups leave.

Already ranked as one of the top ten science museums in the United States, the Hall of Science added to its status in the spring of 1997 when it opened the KIDPOWER Science Playground—the largest in the country. This colorful collection of outdoor educational contraptions is so wildly imaginative, no one under ninety should miss it. High points include a twenty-five-foot seesaw for school group teeter-tottering, a giant pinball machine that kids set off by descending down a slide pole, a sun catcher exhibit using mirrors to aim sunbeams and hit targets, plus a huge elevated energy wave that surfs back and forth for 120 feet. And I'm proud to say I was the first person ever to climb the red rope web of the Space Net tensile structure—to the top!

COOL KID'S CORNER: You'll find a watery exhibit at the Hall of Science where you can make giant bubbles. Here's the same soapy formula they use at the Hall so you can whip up some bubble juice at home: Put 2/3 cup of liquid dishwashing soap (Dawn or Joy are best) in 1 gallon of water. Add 1 tablespoon of glycerine and let the solution age for five days. Presto, bubble mania!

New York Transit Museum

**Address: Corner of Boerum Place
and Schermerhorn Streets, Brooklyn
Phone: 718-243-3060 • Ideal Age Group: 5 to 12
Admission: $3 adults/$1.50 children**

During one of my first excursions into Manhattan, I begged my parents to take me on the subway, such was my fascination with the underground train. I was hooked by the simple novelty of holding my own token and dropping it in the turnstile. When the subway finally rolled into the station, its deafening noise rattled my untrained ears and I freaked out. Luckily, I can now ride the IRT without holding my mother's hand.

Today whenever out-of-town friends visit, their children always want to ride the subway. So we do. We walk up to the front of the first car where we share space with other kids watching the eery black of the subway tunnel racing by.

But I've discovered an even better place for a concentrated dose of subway sensations—the New York Transit Museum. The first hint that this is unlike any museum you've ever seen, is it's location in an authentic, decommissioned IND station in Brooklyn. For the price of a token (double that for you) children can pass through the turnstiles into this subterrranean shrine to commuting.

If you think about it, the subway is an incredible achievement—hundreds of miles of track dug through rock and dirt and mud by 30,000 men using not much more than picks, shovels, and strong immigrant backs. This amazing construction feat is well documented at the Transit Museum, where you can hear stories about diggers sucked out of underground tunnels and blown into the air. But the major attraction here is downstairs in the tube (with its live, 600-watt third rail), the home of nineteen restored subway cars, dating from as far back as 1904 (when a token was 5¢). Kids can ring the bells on wooden cars with wicker seats, or pretend to be traveling to the 1934 World's Fair on cars painted in the official blue and orange exposition colors.

They have some aboveground mass transit vehicles here, too, including the sawed-off cabs from a pair of real New York City buses. Kids clamber up into the driver's seats behind huge steering wheels to peer through the classic fishbowl windows. On the newer bus, I was able to push the overhead route destination buttons with a satisfying high-pitched beep. You'll also find original MTA conductor badges for sale in the gift shop, along with other authentic subway memorabilia and the best collection of children's train books ever gathered in one place.

COOL KID'S CORNER: Before they had subways in Brooklyn, horses pulled buses along tracks. These fast-moving omnibuses were dangerous to passing pedestrians who often had to leap out of the way, earning Brooklyn residents the name Dodgers. You guessed it—that's what they called Brooklyn's only professional baseball team until 1958 when they became the Los Angeles Dodgers.

New York Waterway Cruises

Address: Pier 78 at West 38th Street on the Hudson River
Phone: 1-800-533-3779 • Ideal Age Group: 5 to 12
Admission: $14 adults /$7 children
(No cruises December through March)

C ircumnavigating the city by boat is an excellent way to get an initial overview (or waterview) of this gigantic theme park before immersing kids in the real-life adventure. It's so popular, in fact, that many out-of-town families arriving in New York head directly to the terminals of several river cruise companies docked on the Hudson River.

But I must post a warning. The oldest and best-known of the circle-the-city cruise lines offers a three-hour tour that could have been masterminded by Gilligan for the way it leaves children stranded. Three hours is an awfully long time when you're little. But one new cruise line—New York Waterway Cruises—seems to understand the tolerance level of five to twelve-year-olds, and has created an excursion that abbreviates the trip to a kid-manageable ninety minutes. You won't completely circle Manhattan Island, but you'll enjoy all the highlights children want to see—the Empire State Building, the World Trade Center, the Statue of Liberty, the United Nations complex, and the Brooklyn Bridge.

New York Waterway Cruises also offers a free shuttle

bus service for families staying in midtown that conveniently drops you off at their refurbished terminal at Thirty-eighth Street, where you'll find a number of clean, comfortable, modern ferries. As the boat departs, take a seat on the left side of the upper deck (outside deck if it's sunny) for the best views of the passing skyline.

Knowledgeable and friendly guides pack a lot of fascinating city history into the sight-seeing tour, with just enough silly trivia to hold a child's interest. And I like this cruise for another reason. A lot of tourists feel compelled to take their kids to the Statue of Liberty; but, frankly, I think it's a destination that parents think kids should like, but few children actually do. The lines for both the Liberty Island Ferry and to climb the statue stairs are unbearably long, and you can consume an entire afternoon dragging around a child who's growing justifiably agitated. Most kids are content to see the Green Lady up close from the decks of a New York Waterway Cruise, without stretching the limits of their fidgetiness on the crowded shores of Liberty Island.

COOL KID'S CORNER: Here's some of that silly trivia I was telling you about—did you know that if you take a Hudson River pier number and subtract forty, you can tell what street you're on? Or that the district name, Tribeca, stands for triangle below Canal Street? Or that the Brooklyn Bridge was built in 1883—ten years before cars were invented? I learned a lot on my New York Waterway Cruise.

Niketown

Address: 6 East 57th Street bet. Fifth and Madison Avenues
Phone: 891-6453 • Ideal Age Group: 7 to 12
Admission: Free

I have a Greek friend living in New York who calls his eight- and twelve-year-old nephews overseas to ask them what they want from America. Their answer is always the same— "Nikes!"

If they ever visit New York, these boys will likely join thousands of other sports-loving kids and adults turning Niketown into a major midtown attraction—and for good reason. This is an incredibly cool store built like a 1950s Manhattan school gymnasium (the fictional P.S. 6453), complete with hugh scoreboard, old wooden gym floors, wrestling mats hanging from the walls and banners from the ceiling.

But Nike, arguably the world's most innovative retailer, has married these classic athletic icons with futuristic features like a morphing store interior; every twenty minutes the roof skylight closes, the interior lights dim in the five-story atrium, and a colossal thirty six-by-twenty two-foot media screen drops out of the ceiling. Now hang on for a series of thrilling three-minute films complete with air crackling surround sound. Honestly, I got chills watching these inspiring sports stories.

On all five floors of this amazing retail theater, there are half a dozen highlights that offer nonstop entertainment for kids. Like the space age NGAGE foot-sizing machine that uses a digital camera to measure a person's foot, then spits out a little card you can keep with your exact heel-to-toe specs. There's a genuine heavy bag that you're invited to clobber. Or check out the trophy displays on the second floor containing historic treasures like Carl Lewis' Olympic gold medals, Barry Sanders' 1988 Heisman Trophy, Bernie Williams' World Series bat, and lots more exciting memorabilia.

The big silver vista viewfinders on the fifth floor play two exhilirating short films that put you in the shoes of a streaking mountain biker or a blazing in-line skater. And wait until you see the shoe tubes used at Niketown to transport merchandise from the basement—they were actually inspired by the Jetson's cartoon series! Even a trip to the dressing room here is exciting—I went in to try on a pair of sweatpants and found myself face-to-face with Arvydas Sabonis' size eighteen basketball sneakers sitting in a small wall case display. The Nike swoosh logo on his sneakers was bigger than my whole foot.

COOL KID'S CORNER: Keep your eyes open because Niketown is a regular shopping spot for major celebrity athletes, and that's no hype. Yankee Derek Jeter was here the day he won 1996 Rookie of the Year, the Giants football players often stop in, and many more professional Nike athletes make this their place to shop for "Air" everything.

The Panorama of the City of New York

Address: Queens Museum of Art,
Flushing Meadows Corona Park, Queens
Phone: 718-592-9700 ● Ideal Age Group: 7 to 12
Admission: $3 adults, $1.50 children

Imagine taking the entire City of New York—all five boroughs, every one of the 895,000 buildings, the parks, the rivers, the airports, the thirty-five major bridges—and shrinking it down to fit inside one big room. That's exactly what they did at the Panorama of the City of New York—the world's largest three-dimensional scale model, and an exact replica of Gotham.

The Panorama is simply so awesome that any child who has ever labored over a Legos creation approaches it with dropped jaw and wide eyes. It took 200 model makers, engineers, and draftsmen three years to build the Panorama, originally constructed as an exhibit for the 1964 World's Fair. The cityscape was updated in 1994 by the original builders (Lester & Associates) to include 60,000 changes and additions—so it probably includes your new condominium, too.

At the World's Fair, 1,400 visitors a day viewed the expanse from tracked cars (one of which is on display) that simulated helicopter flight at heights of 3,000 to 20,000 feet. Now you walk along an elevated ramp way with glass floors that runs along the perimeter of the 9,335 square foot model. One of the Panorama's best features, which always elicits oohs and ahhs from young visitors, is the Night Scene enhancement. Every few minutes the room lights dim and the city glows with 2,500 green, orange, red, and blue lights, augmented with special black light illumination. The entire effect is totally eery and wonderful.

The first thing city kids will want to do is find their apartment building and their school, along with landmarks like Yankee Stadium, the Empire State Building (just fifteen inches tall at this 1 inch to 100-foot scale), and the Statue of Liberty (look below your feet along the west walkway). If you want an improved view for both big and little eyes, rent binoculars from the gift shop for $1—it's worth it.

COOL KID'S CORNER: There are three great things to look for while you're here: the miniature airplanes taking off and landing at La Guardia airport—see if you can follow them flying across the night sky of the ceiling, too; the world's largest elevator— located in the lobby of the building, it was used to carry World's Fair tourists visiting the Panorama, and it's the size of a small apartment. Finally, pick up the cool New York Story pop-up toy in the gift shop and hold Manhattan in the palm of your hand!

Playground for All Children

Address: 111-01 Corona Avenue, Flushing Meadows
Corona Park, Queens • Phone: 718-699-8283
Ideal Age Group: 2 to 12 • Admission: Free

When the Playground for All Children (PAC, for short) opened in 1984, it was the first outdoor facility in the world designed to provide integrated play for nondisabled children and children with disabilities. Built at a cost of $3.7 million, this was a showplace facility, the prototype for playgrounds of its kind.

The blueprint was to be repeated in all five boroughs, but funds dried up and PAC remained the only specialized playground in the city until the 1992 opening of the **Asser Levy Recreation Center** in Manhattan (23rd Street at Asser Levy Place/447-2020). While providing a vital service, Asser Levy does not have the range of offerings available at PAC.

"All children" means that the PAC playground has something for all kids, regardless of variation in age or abilities. In fact, you would be unable to distinguish most of the playground apparatus here from equipment in your own neighborhood park, unless you were a child with a disability. Then you would notice that the slide has special wide steps and low railings you can climb with arms only. You would appreciate the nature trail with signs in braille that describe the foliage and points of interest. You would realize that your wheelchair can go anywhere in this 3.5-acre play facility with, of course, unobstructed and easy access to the restrooms.

There are at least two attendants at all times. They understand the needs of these children, focus only on what they *can* do, are trained to provide extra assistance if necessary, and encourage every child to participate fully, no matter what the disability. The staff is particularly skilled at creating games and activities where healthy interaction and integration occurs between nondisabled and disabled children. It's not uncommon to see nondisabled kids pushing wheelchair-bound visitors around the base paths in a pickup game of softball, or cooperative art projects being created at the indoor crafts area.

Other highlights of this playground include four hand-operated swings with adult-sized seats—these aluminium and rubber, high-back chairs have foot restraints and seat belts, and can be pumped with a pull chain. There are also puppet shows starring disabled puppets in the amphitheater during summer months and an immensely popular Water Wheel—a fully accessible wet play area that douses delighted kids in July and August.

COOL KID'S CORNER: When you visit here, you might see one of the PAC Pack—six dogs used in an innovative Pet Assisted Therapy program at the playground. These gentle canines can push wheelchairs, help kids on apparatus, and offer lots of love. Ask to meet Frieda, the blind German Shepherd, or the playground favorite, Ayla, who actually responds to commands given in sign language!

Playspace

Address: 2473 Broadway at 92nd Street
Phone: 769-2300 • Ideal Age Group: 2 to 6
Admission: $4.50 per adult/$4.50 per child/2nd adult free

J ump, run, crawl, slide, skip, tumble, dig, push, wriggle, laugh, climb, touch, share, eat, peek, sing, tickle, hug, hum, hop. Well, that about sums up the life of a toddler, and gives you a good idea of what to expect at the city's best indoor playground for the under six crowd.

What makes Playspace so superior? You'll like it for the helpful staff (they'll run out and buy a fresh pair of OshKosh in the wake of a hopeless soiling), the immaculate cleanliness (toys are sterilized every night), the premium put on safety, and the natural bright light from floor-to-ceiling windows. Your child won't notice any of that—in fact, I predict a bee-line to the huge sandbox (5,000 pounds of the white stuff, strained and sifted nightly), the colorful elevated labyrinth, the miniature stage loaded with tutus and dress-up costumes, and the lock, latch, and hatch-covered Door Wall (finally, three-year-olds get to bust open every throw bolt and twist lock known to man).

Another reason why Playspace is so much fun for kids, while accommodating the needs of escorting parents, is that this 8,000 square foot play area was designed by a parent, not a business person. Owner and creator Allen McCullough was at a loss some years back when his son needed a safe, clean, rain-or-shine alternative to apartment play. The Vermont native wanted to capture the best of small-town life and employed master playground builder, Sam Kornhauser, to make this concept a reality.

The two men actually sawed and hammered much of the natural wood play areas themselves, mixing special nontoxic stains to create soothing wine and mustard-color motifs on exposed panels. The two levels of the handmade, suspended crawl bridge have lots of built-in secret places and kid-sized crannies to hide in. McCullough and Kornhauser tested all the crawl spaces themselves to insure that parents could accompany toddlers through every tunnel and climbing structure—another one of those safety-first features that includes a couple of inches of rubber surfacing on the floors and thick carpet padding everywhere else.

But let's get back to the sheer joy of unstructured play for preschoolers. There are dozens of popular riding toys in the parking lot, a light booth where kinetic kids can throw the flicker switch like crazy, a tree house, a bilevel construction area with a neat wrecking ball, and (I love this) the city's smallest climbing wall—very short and blanketed with carpet so you can leave your safety harnesses at home.

COOL KID'S CORNER: How much sand can you stand? The very big sandbox at Playspace is filled with digging trucks, special sifters on the wall, plus all the pails, shovels, and rakes you can hold. If you want to play alone, the sandbox has a private clubhouse and a cozy foam cave in the corner.

The Puppet Company

Address: 31 Union Square West at 16th Street, Loft 2B
Phone: 741-1646 • Ideal Age Group: 2 to 10
Admission: $7.50 per person
Saturday and Sunday shows only, reservations required

In the world of puppetry, it is said that every puppet has a soul, and it's the soul of the puppeteer. If that's true, then the imaginative, finely crafted, lovable puppets created by Steve Widerman at The Puppet Company would have to be the most soulful in the city.

New York has a number of professional venues where children can experience excellent puppet theater every weekend of the year. **PuppetWorks** ($5 children/338 Sixth Avenue at 4th Street, Park Slope/718-965-3391), under the skilled direction of Nick Coppola, is locally famous for thirty-five years of traditional marionette productions at its storefront theater in Brooklyn's historic district. You're also guaranteed a polished, wonderfully varied performance by world-class puppeteers at the beautiful **Lenny Suib Puppet Playhouse** at Asphalt Green ($3.50 children/555 East 90th Street at York Avenue/369-8890).

But your child will never feel more given to than at one of the intimate performances by Mr. Widerman in his kid-proportioned, thirty-five-seat loft theater at Union Square. A protégé of legendary puppet master, Bil Baird, Steve began fooling around with puppets at the age of seven and never stopped. He and his sister, Susan, opened the company in 1977 and launched their first public performances in 1988.

Steve crafts every puppet you see himself, whether it's a wood-carved marionette (some evolving over two years), a finger puppet, or a Celastic hand puppet, and he considers each a sculpture. With his deft manipulation, the beautifully made and meticulously detailed puppet characters have a beguiling and enchanting presence on stage, magical enough to hold the attention of even the youngest fans. Every new show (the season lasts from October through April) also includes lively piano music, all written and performed by the University of Pennsylvania trained Widerman.

Because he realizes that his puppet performances are often a child's first exposure to theater of any kind, Steve and his troupe plan every minute of the humorous, hour-long shows in detail, always incorporating opportunities for audience participation. Steve even emerges during each performance to demonstrate the making of a simple puppet—a cute Lampchop-like sock puppet, for instance, or an old racquetball cut in two with pushpin eyes.

So take your children over to The Puppet Company. Let Steve show them how to create puppets at home. Then lock up your socks.

COOL KID'S CORNER: After the performance, ask Steve to bring out his famous, funniest puppet characters, like the amiable Al E. Gator, the singing Gum Rappers trio, the new Mr. Ritz, and Burnadette the dragon who can't stand smoke!

The Real World

Address: Rockefeller Park, Chambers Street
on the Hudson River
Phone: 416-5300 • Ideal Age Group: 2 to 12
Admission: Free

E very so often, an artist is born who can live a lifetime without losing the instincts to create like a child. The imagination stays nimble and fresh. A playfulness remains. For those exceptional people, the world of fantasy is comfortable and real . . . while reality seems ridiculous.

Tom Otterness is just that sort of artist. And his Real World playground of absurd and comical creatures in Rockefeller Park speaks the visual language of children perfectly. It is impossible to dislike Otterness' fairy-tale family of pint-sized busy bodies—a civilization of bronze smiley faces I call the "Pill Box" men (because of those hats). Swimming in a sea of oversized pennies—the artist's reference to nearby Wall Street—these and all sorts of half-human, half-animal carnivalesque sculptures delight children of every age in their riverfront tiny town.

Otterness is a Kansas native (possible Oz influence here) whose highly recognizable sculptures have been commissioned for projects throughout the city, including an underworld creation for the Mass Transit Authority.

He likes to make public art because it reaches so many people. He works in bronze because he says it gets polished when people touch it—that way he can tell which of his sculptures children love most. His genial Dodo bird is frequently nuzzled by countless toddlers just a few hundred yards away in the Rockefeller Playground (see page 90).

He's created so many crazy characters in the Real World, doing so many offbeat things, your eyes have to work overtime. At the north entrance, you'll spot a bulldog chained to a water fountain, barking at a cat who's watching a bird who's eyeing a worm. Over there is Humpty Dumpty on the violin. Nearby, two frogs are wrestling under a penny fountain. And everywhere the Pill Box men are making mischief.

You'll discover that the Real World is particularly well-suited to young children learning their numbers. There's a long winding Penny Path snaking through the playground with an alternating little feet motif. Children can step on the feet while counting pennies along the walkway for a game that fully engages little minds and bodies.

COOL KID'S CORNER: Mr. Otterness has tucked some of his most magical sculptures in hard-to-see places. Can you find the cigar-smoking turtle on the wall, the dark monk with a sickle sitting atop a light post, the gagged cat, the unplugged phone, and the man-snake reading on the pole? The first one to find all five wins!

Rockefeller Playground

**Address: Rockefeller Park, Vesey Street on the
Hudson River • Phone: 416-5300
Ideal Age Group: 2 to 10 • Admission: Free**

During research for this book, I spoke to dozens of parents and children about their favorite places to visit in New York. An astonishing number of fun-seeking informants named the Rockefeller Playground "the city's best playground." One family was so hooked, they visited regularly from Brooklyn to play here on weekends.

How, I wondered, could one cluster of slides, sandboxes, and jungle gyms gain such unanimous praise and stand so far above the rest? I went to find out—and I had to forcibly restrain myself from throwing off my jacket and dashing up the red climbing nets. Why do six-year-olds have all the fun?

One of the outstanding features of this playground is its idyllic setting on the waterfront, within twenty five acres of continuous parks and gardens. This open, airy environment just steps from the surging Hudson, basks children in sunlight and sea breeze and contributes to an expansive play experience. In a city where children are too often confined to small, limited play areas, Rockefeller Playground says "you're free, go wild." And kids do.

To my eye, the playground is built as a microcosm of

the city—with a maze of high-rise climbing structures, bridges, and towers looking down on the bustling activity of toddler play areas, hopscotch games and sandboxes. This playground is also so safe, clean, and smartly designed, parents find they can temporarily relax their own vigilance and just let kids play. Opportunities abound for that.

At the south end is a cheerful red carousel for smaller children that parents can push or kids can pedal power. It travels slowly on its own circular track and always prompts a passing parade of smiling faces. Further on is a wooden-bowed bridge (run fast, make lots of banging sounds with your feet), firemen's sliding poles, a bright yellow spiral slide, a three-foot elevated sandbox for standing play, lots of swings, muscle-building climbing nets, and several springy jumpers. The expansive climbing area is clearly marked (9 AND OLDER, AGES 2–5, etc.), so parents can gauge apparatus difficulty with a child's skill level. The entire playground is also covered with a thick, spongy surface to cushion inevitable falls.

This state-of-the-art playground includes an amusing water play area where a big concrete hippo faces off with a undaunted elephant in a summer-long squirting duel. Four dog faces peer out of the adjacent east wall to get in on the spouting fun.

COOL KID'S CORNER: Bring your chalk. The bouncy black surface of the playground is really fun to draw on. Everywhere you look children have created chalk flowers, houses, colorful hopping paths, and chalk people, too.

Roosevelt Island Aerial Tram

Address: 59th Street and Second Avenue
Phone: 832-4543 • Ideal Age Group: 3 to 8
Admission: $3 round-trip

When you're looking for great places to take children, you've got to think like a child. Let's take the Roosevelt Island Tram, for instance. Now to most adults it's a practical, if not picturesque way to commute between the East River island and Manhattan. But to a kid, the tram is a carnival ride, a bubble in the sky, a great way to fly!

Every fifteen minutes the aerial tram departs from Sixtieth Street and starts its three-and-a-half minute glide, 250 feet above the river on huge cables. For children, this experience is a major rush. The large, four-sided glass cable cars offer a way-up-high view of the towering skyscrapers of midtown. Kids love to watch the multicolored specks racing down the black ribbons of the avenues, while chubby tug-boats push barges through the swirling river waters below.

There are a thousand things to see from the Roosevelt Island Tram and children capture it all: cars zipping by on the adjacent Queensboro Bridge, helicopters taking off from the Sixty-third Street Heliport, a police boat plying the waters near the Manhattan shoreline, a building fire trailing smoke somewhere far off in Brooklyn.

After this aerial sight-seeing tour is over, the tram follows a steep slope into its docking descent and jerks to rest with a few bumps that always amuse little ones. Once off the cable car, walk your children over to the big window of the tram's engine room. You can peek inside to see the enormous yellow gears and the blue, orange, and green Tinker Toy interior. Was this place made for kids or what?

Don't quit now. This is a fun-filled little island which starts with a 25¢ ride on the red buses along Main Street. Ride to the northernmost stop where you and your children can step off, then continue to walk past the beautiful community gardens along the East River promenade to the child-sized, fifty-foot stone lighthouse at the island's tip. There's a wonderful sun-filled park for picnicking here, a fine place for quiet conversation with your kids (remember that?) away from the bustle of Manhattan. You'll probably see a handful of friendly fisherman and lots of seagulls but few other island dwellers. The native Canarsie Indians called this little island Minnahannock, loosely translated as "It's Nice to Be on the Island." Yeah, sure, but who would want to miss the return ride to Manhattan on the tram?

COOL KID'S CORNER: Here's my favorite thing to do on the aerial tram. Watch for the other cable car passing by in the opposite direction. You'll meet at about midpoint and then you can make friendly, funny faces at the huddled commuters floating by!

Smithsonian's National Museum of the American Indian

Address: 1 Bowling Green, across from Battery Park
Phone: 668-6624 • Ideal Age Group: 6 to 12
Admission: Free

I have always been moved by the Native American philosophy regarding the seventh generation—that whatever we do today, we should consider its impact on the seventh generation of our children. It's probably naive to romanticize the traditions of indigenous peoples, but they do have something to teach us about the delicate balance between people and nature, spirituality and art, and respect for family.

At the beautifully curated American Indian museum, children are exposed to some of the intricate crafts, powerful music, old stories, and native objects that say so much about the people of these fascinating cultures. These exhibits are made even more riveting and dramatic by the museum's location in a magnificent landmark building—the old U.S. Custom House, a Beaux Arts masterpiece built just after the turn of the century (mention to your children that the main rotunda on the second floor, with its oval skylight and detailed ceiling murals, is used in many Hollywood movies).

The Smithsonian has more than one million Native

American artifacts in its collection with only a small number on display here. Still, there's no shortage of stone carvings, weavings, baskets, pottery, and jewelry in the winding galleries. Leather fighting shields, feathered war bonnets, and frightful dance masks always get a child's attention, although much of these items appear behind glass cases, off-limits to curious young hands. There are a few touchable items, most notably a thick buffalo-skin robe which evokes snowy scenes from *Dances with Wolves*. I also like the constant chanting and drumming of tribal music piped through the space, which heightens the mystery and intensity.

Very young children will tire quickly of the artifacts displays, which require easy but sometimes extensive reading. They'll be happier in front of the video screens featuring legends, myths, and stories told by contemporary chiefs and elders, both men and women. The Resource Center also has five interactive touch screens with age-appropriate activities. Finally, the museum features an Especially For Kids film series twice a day, focusing on the lives of today's Native American youngsters.

I saw the largest number of children clustered near the Round Dance Exhibit, a display incorporating dozens of pairs of colorfully-beaded moccasins, all arranged in a circle, left foot up, as if the wearers were midstep in a ritual powwow dance. It gave me chills.

COOL KID'S CORNER: You can buy authentic Native American turquoise jewelry and silver work, beaded vests, feathered headdresses, and drumming music in the gift shop. Also, visit the Resource Center where they have tribal newspapers like the *Navajo Times* and *Seminole Tribune* sent from reservations.

Socrates Sculpture Park

**Address: Broadway at Vernon Boulevard,
Long Island City, Queens • Phone: 718-956-1819
Ideal Age Group: 5 to 12 • Admission: Free**

Too much art in too many pretentious settings can discourage a kid. I had the misfortune of plunking myself down in a giant leather Claes Oldenburg baseball mitt at the Guggenheim not long ago, and was soundly chastised by a passing museum guard (she actually called me a "dummy"). Hey, I couldn't help it, the impulse just came over me.

No such problem for energetic souls at the Socrates Sculpture Park. Children of all ages are encouraged to touch, hang from, climb over, and sit on dozens of large scale sculptures in this 4.5-acre waterfront park. The inspiration of Queens steel girder sculptor, Mark di Suvero, this unassuming sculpture garden was an illegal garbage dump for years, until it was reclaimed and revitalized by the artist and his neighbors in 1985.

Not that Socrates Park has forgotten it's humble beginnings. You can still find a piece of rusted wire here, a butane tank in the bushes over there, an old oil drum tossed by a storm fence. But overall, the former rubble-strewn lot offers a kind of rugged sanctuary from the oily garages, welding shops, and masonry warehouses on Vernon Boulevard. It's okay to run, play, throw a ball, or picnic in the shadow of

Socrates' towering wood, stone, and steel creations by both well-known and emerging artists. It's a particularly smart excursion with children on hot days when the East River breezes cool off the shoreline and circulate the five melodious tones of the windmill-like sculpture titled Wind Gamelan.

Feeling climby? Two curious sculptures, the satellite silhouette of The Cloak of Motion and the neon green top of the aluminium and Plexiglas Resurrection bridge, rival the best outdoor playground apparatus. Children always spot the green, wood-carved snake slithering up the sculpted tree above Socrates' office trailer, too—just another inch and it will finally gulp down that egg. Another favorite pastime for children here is locating their initials in the granite alphabet wall that borders the park on the east side. Exhibits change with regularity, too, so there's always something new looming before you.

Besides its dramatic physical setting, and the interactive nature of its sculptures, Socrates is unusual in another respect. Children have the opportunity to meet artists working on-site. Watching sculptors create their pieces with rock-crushing jackhammers and white-hot torches never fails to impress kids who tend to believe that all art is made in genteel studios with delicate tools.

COOL KID'S CORNER: Along the eastern fence of Socrates Park lies the sculpture, Vanishing, with 300 endangered species pictured on ceramic tile blocks—everything from frogs to deer to ducks to snakes to shellfish. See how many different animals you can find and name, or bring your school class here to identify imperiled species you'll help protect one day.

Sony 3-D IMAX Theatre

Address: 68th Street at Broadway
Phone: 336-5000 • Ideal Age Group: 6 to 12
Admission: $9 adults /$6 children

Everything at the Sony IMAX Theatre is big. And kids love big. There's a big movie screen (largest in the country, second largest on the planet), a big sound system (18,000 watts of surround sound), and big 3-D action (stampeding buffalos as big as bulldozers, frolicking fish the size of freighters). Just taking the escalators past the seventy-five-foot Hollywood mural up to the 600-seat theatre is a big experience.

But, without a doubt, the coolest part of IMAX for children is the futuristic headsets they issue you as you step through the theatre door. Forget those outdated scenes from the 1950s of a stiff, formally dressed audience watching 3-D movies wearing cardboard sunglasses. Totally unique to this theatre location is a lightweight, heavy-duty pair of plastic goggles that look like a marriage between a welder's mask and virtual reality headgear. With my pair firmly over my face I felt like Luke Skywalker in *Star Wars,* and I didn't want to take them off (but I had to—each pair gets a thorough cleaning and disinfecting before the next show begins).

Once you've finished laughing at the bizarre look these wraparound 3-D headsets give the rest of the family, you can lean back in the comfy seats for the IMAX movie. IMAX is the world's largest film format (ten times larger than 35mm) which enables the theatre to project a monstrous image onto a screen the size of an eight-story building—eighty-feet high by one hundred-feet wide. Add the advanced 3-D technology, and you're sitting at the edge of your seat watching movie images that surround you, crawl into your lap, almost sneak up behind you. Invariably, you also see lots of little hands reaching out to snatch passing 3-D images from the air (okay, I did it, too).

For non-English-speaking families, the Sony IMAX Theatre offers many of their 3-D movies in your choice of five languages: Japanese, Spanish, German, French, and English. Recent films like the cosmic L5—*First City in Space,* the nostalgic *Across the Sea of Time,* and the underwater adventure *Into the Deep* can all be selected in these multilingual versions.

COOL KID'S CORNER: Besides showing big 3-D movies, this Sony Theatre complex is also the site of big movie premieres. My nephew, Zach, was up from Florida once when we saw Eddie Murphy pull up in a long black stretch limo for a movie opening here. Eddie walked right up to him, winked, and shook his hand. Zach told everybody about it for weeks and still says it was the best thing that ever happened to him in New York.

Sony Wonder Technology Lab

Address: 550 Madison Avenue at 56th Street
Phone: 833-8100 • Ideal Age Group: 6 to 12
Admission: Free

Connecting high tech with high touch is the idea behind Sony Wonder, where children become media trainees and get to explore all the newest eye-popping communications technology coming out of the company's cutting edge computer and video labs.

It's hard to imagine that Sony would assemble this futuristic cyber station in the first place, much less make it available free to the public. But here it is, four floors of on-line playground and digital adventure, and if Sony wants to throw in a few plugs for its products for the visitation privileges, that's cool with me.

You're greeted at the ground floor elevators by young Sony staffers (called "Explainers") clad in black jumpsuits with walkie-talkies and headsets, and already you're hooked by the promise of something sensational. Next you're handed a Sony Wonder Card and whisked up to the Log-In Station—a kind of darkened, intergalactic star world rigged with eight video prompts. At log-in you hear a chorus of male and female voices beckoning you to the video screens, "Come here, over here." Then you follow your on-screen guides to have the Wonder Card magnetically encoded with your name, image, and voice imprint. The card now becomes your pass for activating exhibits. (Hint: When the camera locks onto your image, make a funny face for repeated laughs every time you swipe the card.)

Yahoo! Now you can descend the chrome and neon ramps into three more floors of fun. First I stopped at ROVER (Remote Operated Video Enhanced Robot) to manipulate a giant robotic arm in an attempt to find a dangerous radioactive leak—I broke a sweat. Next it was on to the Audio Lab, where I sat at a jazzy console with other media trainees and created a bizarre musical composition. Then, at the Image Lab, my funny face was projected on a screen before me, and using a handheld Power Tracker gun, I electronically painted, pinched, and ultimately turned my image into a monstrous mosaic.

Sony Wonder Technology Lab also has a digital recording studio where kids can reengineer part of a pop music sound track, as well as a working television studio that gives children a chance to play camera operator and director. But the ultimate charge for most kids is the PlayStation, an area stocked with the latest 3-D video games. After being KO'd repeatedly in an incredibly realistic kung-fu kicking duel, I reluctantly handed over my joystick to an eight-year-old breathing down my neck.

COOL KID'S CORNER: Say hello to B. B. Wonderbot, the bug-eyed, remote-controlled robot who'll meet you at the entrance to Sony Wonder. B. B. has miniature television cameras hidden in his eyeballs and microphones implanted in his faceless head to see and hear all. Once inside the lab, you'll see the operator who controls this amusing, lifelike robot using virtual reality gadgetry.

South Street Seaport Buskers

Address: 19 Fulton Street
Phone: 732-7678 • Ideal Age Group: 2 to 12
Admission: Free to marketplace/Fees vary for museums

The recent revitalization of lower Manhattan is one of the city's most impressive achievements, offering families a fascinating square mile of fulfilling outings: there are the four, well-marked Heritage Trails for exploring the Colonial settlement of New Amsterdam; a rich schedule of summer-long free family performances in Hudson and Battery Parks; or for a mere 50¢ round-trip, you can take your child on a scenic, hour-long boat ride through New York Harbor aboard the big orange and blue Staten Island Ferry.

But for sheer entertainment, there's no better bet than a visit to the eleven square blocks of restored nineteenth century buildings known as the South Street Seaport. Dating back to the 1600s, the Seaport district now draws more than 10 million people a year to its maritime museum, street-level retail shops, and thirty-five restaurants. There's a small Children's Center with hands-on exhibits all related to waterfront life and sea voyaging where kids can rock on a heavy mast to experience the fury of strong seas. Children of every age are also drawn to the Seaport's historic tall ships. Climb aboard the landmark *Peking*—a 347-foot, four-masted giant that's the second-largest sailing ship in the world today. Or cast off for a two-hour sail on the century-old schooner *Pioneer*, where children can help raise the sails or even take the helm (the *Pioneer* sails seasonally).

But, in my opinion, the single most appealing children's attraction at the Seaport is the incredible concentration of buskers, or street artists. During the warm months, the Seaport encourages street performers to entertain along the cobblestone pedestrian walkways, and these talented artists arrive in droves. What results is an amazingly vibrant carnival, a street circus, a colorful world of jugglers, magicians, mimes, musicians, puppeteers, and balloonists. And all this entertainment is free.

One summer Sunday I listened to a guitarist play a medley of Neil Young tunes, a magician struggle to rip himself free of a straitjacket in under two minutes, an acrobat juggle knives while another swallowed fire, and a comedian do twenty minutes of G-rated material. In fact, the children were laughing hardest.

COOL KID'S CORNER: Look for the green-painted lady posing as a stone still Statue of Liberty, the young piano virtuoso playing Beethoven on a portable keyboard while his father collects the change, and the silent balloon sculptor skillfully twisting rubber animals for a dollar. There are so many weird and wacky buskers at the Seaport, you may have to come back again tomorrow.

TADA!

Address: 120 West 28th Street, 2nd floor,
bet. Sixth and Seventh Avenues
Phone: 627-1732 • Ideal Age Group: 5 to 12
Admission: 8-week classes start at $175

This is a city for entertainers, with hundreds of Broadway plays, cabarets, staged readings, and musical concerts going up every night. Talented actors, singers, dancers, and performers of every size, shape, and vocal range are giving their all to make audiences laugh, cry, and vibrate with excitement. It's electrifying stuff, and if you're a little person growing up here you can't help but be infected; you've got to wonder if maybe, just maybe, there isn't a little bit of star in you.

Well raise the curtain and turn on the footlights, because I know the perfect place to find out—TADA! This unique theater company and performance school gives kids a place to develop their voice, dance, and stage techniques in a safe, supportive, upbeat environment. And TADA is exclusively for children—in fact, it's New York's only youth theater ensemble, with classes and productions that are relevant to kids.

Young performers from every ethnic and socioeconomic background come here to hone dramatic skills, learn improvisation, and play theater games (in the five-to-six-year-old classes, children also make simple masks, props, and puppets to use in shows). And as it turns out, many of the city's finest professional actors aren't waiting tables, they're teaching at TADA. Every after-school and Saturday class (maximum of twenty children) is taught by a choreographer and a musical director, along with one college-age theater intern—so even the more introverted students get attention.

Each class semester ends with an exuberant performance for families and friends in TADA's very own ninety-five-seat theater (hey, this is show biz). Many children in the musical theater school then try out in open auditions to become a member of TADA's ensemble troupe, which puts on three high-quality, original productions a year.

Watching a class of eight to twelve-year-olds in TADA's rehearsal space, I was reminded of a humiliating experience I had in the third grade singing an "Edelweiss" solo in an assembly. I thought I'd pulled it off quite well, but was later mocked by the music teacher for a few squeals on the high notes. End of singing career. You can be sure there's nothing like that going on at TADA. The instructors I saw were positively thrilled with every sung note and dance step, and the kids all seemed to shine in the generous spotlight. I was also amazed at the camaraderie between these preteens, with the more confident kids pulling the wallflowers, well . . . off the wall.

COOL KID'S CORNER: I thought you might like to hear part of a poem written by a kid like you who was excited to be performing at TADA, "I shouted, I screamed, I strutted, I pranced, did cartwheels and flips and sang and danced, for I had just gotten the best news so far, that I would belong to a place called, TADA!"

Tannen's Magic Studio

**Address: 24 West 25th Street bet.
Sixth Avenue and Broadway, 2nd floor
Phone: 929-4500 ● Ideal Age Group: 5 to 12
Admission: Free**

Hocus Pocus! Abracadabra! Simsalabim! These are the magic words. Children all over the world learn them almost as soon as they can talk, and everytime they're spoken there's the anticipation of something strange about to happen, something amazing and wonderful.

As it turns out, the world's epicenter for constant quakes of magical excitement is right here in New York, at Tannen's Magic Studio. The largest magic shop on the planet, with more than 7,800 tricks, gags, and illusions in stock, has been a mecca for amateur and professional magicians for more than sixty years. New Jersey native, David Copperfield, got his start at Tannen's purchasing card tricks as a teenager. Siegfried and Roy bought their first illusions from Tannen's owner, Tony Spina, thirty years ago. Dick Cavett, a master at sleight of hand, is a regular customer. Even Muhammed Ali, a magic nut, shops here.

For children, a visit to Tannen's is like every birthday party they've ever been to rolled into one. The moment they step into the store, they are surrounded, floor to ceiling, with the countless colorful props that make every magic show so unforgettable—silk scarves, magic wands, shiny coins, big top hats, mysterious black boxes, startling straitjackets, razor sharp swords, dangling ropes, and decks upon decks of rigged playing cards. Even the most jaded child could spend an hour here transfixed by the mesmerizing faces of the ventriloquist dummies in the front display case.

And there's an added bonus with every trip to Tannen's—a free magic show. You see, Tony Spina and all the folks behind the counter are professional magicians. From morning til night, they demonstrate the coin magic, illusions, and card tricks that prospective customers have come to buy. And kids can watch.

Tannen's has some excellent beginner magic sets for children seven and older that offer a dozen simple tricks for under $30. Three marvelous tricks you can ask for—magic that kids love and can master easily—are Spooky (the floating spirit silk), Scotch 'N Soda (a half dollar and copper coin switch), and the Magic Coloring Book. My suggestion is that you let younger children enjoy the illusion of magic as long as possible, and leave the starter sets for slightly older kids.

COOL KID'S CORNER: Look up when you enter Tannen's. See all those playing cards stuck to the ceiling. They're part of an unbelievable trick called "Card on the Ceiling," which the staff magicians will perform for you. And when you get a little older, you'll be ready to learn other famous tricks on sale here, like the Bohemian Torture Escape, Twisting Head, Girl into Lion, and the Buzz Saw Illusion!

Winnie-the-Pooh
at Donnell Library Center

Address: 20 West 53rd Street bet. Fifth and Sixth Avenues
Phone: 212-621-0636 • Ideal Age Group: 2 to 12
Admission: Free

I didn't discover the reassuring sweetness of the Winnie-the-Pooh books until I was in my late twenties. My life had become anxiety filled and difficult, and I was feeling small and frightened. Quite by accident, I stumbled upon A. A. Milne's 1920s children's classics, and read myself to sleep with Pooh and his friends for months. The Bear with Little Brain made me smile, and Piglet's tiny vulnerability made me cry. I could sympathize with Eeyore's gloominess because I was feeling the same way, while I longed for Tigger's bounciness and Kanga's mothering. Spending time in the calming rhythms of the Hundred Acre Wood healed me, and I'm grateful for it.

What's quite astonishing is that many children today don't realize that the hero of the series, Christopher Robin, was the actual son of A. A. Milne, and that his cherished stuffed animal family was quite real. What's even more amazing is that five of Christoper Robin's original toy companions (including Pooh) left England in 1947 and now live permanently here in New York at the Donnell Library's

Central Children's Room.

You can't help but feel awed and excited as you step off the second floor elevator and approach the famous faces of Tigger, Kanga, Pooh, Eeyore, and Piglet, sitting silently in a climate-controlled glass case. Oh, what I'd give to cuddle that Pooh bear for just a minute or two.

It's clear that Christopher Robin loved his plush pals well—Piglet's fur has been hugged right down to the leather, Kanga's neck has been squeezed so hard it has required several surgeries, and Eeyore wears more than one reparative patch. But it's the sight of Pooh, sitting nobly in the center, that makes your heart skip a beat. Not the Disney animation Pooh, not a cheap stuffed imitation Pooh, but the real Edward Bear Sanders who went bump, bump, bump on the back of his head coming down the stairs behind Christopher Robin. Be sure to sign Pooh's guest book, along with thousands of other children and adult fans from around the world who have already sworn their devotion.

COOL KID'S CORNER: Press your nose to the display glass and look closely at the downcast Eeyore. You'll see a very fine netting over his body applied by museum curators trying to protect the weary gray donkey. Nearby, you can also see the parakeet-topped parasol owned by Mary Poppins creator, P. L. Travers; several rabbit figurines donated by Peter Rabbit author, Beatrix Potter; and original paper cuts by Hans Christian Andersen of Ugly Duckling fame—all part of the enchanting children's book collection housed here.

WonderCamp

Address: 27 West 23rd Street bet. Fifth and Sixth Avenues
Phone: 243-1111 • Ideal Age Group: 2 to 10
Admission: $6.50 per person

You enter through the Gatehouse, take a walk down the
Forest Trail by the Field Stage, then wave to some of your
fellow campers making popsicle stick puppets in the Arts
and Crafts Cabin. You dash past some wild animals, enter
the Club House for singing and dancing with your favorite
counselor, then stroll over to the Canteen for a little grub.

This is day camp, right? Well, sort of. It's actually
WonderCamp—a clean, bright, $2 million approximation
of a summer camp in the middle of Chelsea. A number of
similar pay-for-play indoor spaces have sprung up around
the city recently—a reaction, no doubt, to the growing con-
cerns among parents with city playgrounds. Even the king of
kid centers, Discovery Zone, opened one of its megazones
around the corner, then closed suddenly. Guess this wonder
world was too much for them.

While some might consider the all-out camp theme here
a little kitschy (I was going to say campy), I think it's unique,
well-executed, and lots of fun. Heck, kids love camp, and too
many city kids are without a reference point for the camp
experience. True, you won't find 2,000 acres of forests, fields,
and lakes at WonderCamp, but 20,000 square feet in the

heart of Manhattan leaves lots of room to play.

With all that real estate, WonderCamp is able to put together a full day of diverse and engaging activities for every age group. If your child is into computers, there's a FutureKids Computer Cabin with the latest interactive computer games and educational software. At the Field Stage, kids can learn circus arts like juggling and clowning or create campfire tales with a madlibs-type hilarity. Kid Karaoke is scheduled for the corner Club House, which is equipped with an oversized projection TV and advanced sound system. This is where I watched the *Terrific Trip to the Firehouse* video with some four-year-old friends—we were all glued to the screen.

The friendly, entertaining counselors I observed—all trained in performing arts or early childhood education—were extremely patient and energetic. I was amazed at how many children's names they remembered without the aid of name tags. They're also safety conscious at WonderCamp, using a barcoded wristband security system to keep kids and parents matched up.

COOL KID'S CORNER: WonderCamp has the ultimate indoor climbing maze. The incredible, three-story WonderGym is loaded with more twists, turns, tunnels, and detours than the New York City subway. It's got all the stuff you love—big ball pits, three long multicolored spiral slides, climbing nets, aerial tubes, bumper forests, swinging ropes, and more. The WonderGym is humongous!

10 More
Great Places
for Kids

Just for the Fun of It!

Brooklyn Children's Museum

**Address: 145 Brooklyn Avenue
and St. Mark's Avenue, Brooklyn
Phone: 718-735-4400 • Ideal Age Group: 2 to 12
Admission: $3 per person**

The world's first museum created just for children knows a few things about keeping kids entertained and interested. Founded in 1899, BCM pioneered the concept of participatory exhibits, and kids have had their hands occupied ever since. Noted for its subterranean architecture (from street level, all you see is a bunker-type entrance and some bumps in the lawn), the museum's single most compelling feature is the corrugated metal tunnel—a reclaimed drainage pipe—which descends through four levels of the underground structure. This neon-lit people tube has a 120-foot stream running down its middle with paddle wheels, sluiceways, and water gates that kids can manipulate. A $7 million renovation in 1996 added a rooftop amphitheater, a hands-on science and computer laboratory, and an expanded greenhouse. The greenhouse, in particular, buzzes with activity as urban kids make contact with green growing things, and learn about plants with exploding seeds and weeds that can grow twelve feet a year.

Chinatown Ice Cream Factory

Address: 65 Bayard Street bet. Mott and Elizabeth Streets
Phone: 608-4170 • Ideal Age Group: 2 to 12
Admission: $1.90 per scoop

I f every child's favorite food is pizza, then the favorite dessert has to be ice cream. And the freshest, creamiest, most irresistible ice cream in New York is found right here in this little Chinatown shop. The Seid Brothers (William, Henry, Eugene, Philip, and Otis), make all thirty-two flavors on premises from natural ingredients. The Asian specialties—like ginger, litchi, mango, green tea, and red bean—are buttery and exotic. But on a recent visit, I gorged on a double scoop of almond cookie and banana—the most intensely flavored ice creams I've ever tasted. Philip tells me the current favorites among aficionados are Oreo cookie, coconut fudge, and pineapple. His favorite is pistachio (although he looks like a chocolate chip man to me). If you've walked halfway down Mott Street and realize your kids couldn't possibly live without a frozen dessert fix for another week, ask Philip to pack a take home quart to the brim.

Chuck E. Cheese

**Address: 221 Bergen Mall off Route 4 East,
Paramus, New Jersey**
Phone: 201-587-1353 ● Ideal Age Group: 2 to 8
Admission: Parties start at $8.99 per child

Ask any parent in Northern New Jersey to name the number one birthday party spot and they'll tell you Chuck E. Cheese. The only reason this huge pizza-and-play franchise (300 locations in the United States) hasn't invaded the city is that they need thousands of square feet to do what they do; namely, create a decent pizza joint in a child-friendly, arcade-like atmosphere. Chuck E. himself is a playful mouse on hormones, with big buck teeth and a blue-and-red beanie. The illustrious rodent makes an appearance on the half hour to the approving screams of every pint-sized pizza eater in the place. But the most startling attraction here is the SkyTube, a maze of multicolored tunnels suspended from the ceiling, which you could easily mistake for the ventilation system except for the clusters of kids climbing joyfully through it. Get ready for a weird experience—eating a slice of pizza with toddlers dangling over your head.

Dana Discovery Center

Address: 110th Street near Fifth Avenue
Phone: 860-1370 • Ideal Age Group: 4 to 12
Admission: Free

J ust think of it, you and the kids sitting on the shaded bank of a quiet lake, bamboo fishing poles dangling over the water, large-mouth bass flirting with your bait. Colorado, right? Vermont? No, Manhattan. If you don't believe me, pack a picnic lunch and head to the northernmost end of Central Park. That's where landscape architect Laura Starr joined the Central Park Conservancy to transform the Harlem Meer (an eleven-acre lake) from a debris-filled swamp into a stunning nature area with wetlands, a sandy beach, and a restored brick boathouse. The boathouse is the center of activities for kids year-round, used for environmental education, arts-and-crafts workshops, hands-on science projects and . . . fishing! The lake is stocked with more than 50,000 bass, catfish, shiners, and bluegills for kids to catch and release. The poles, the bait, and all the enriching kids' programs here are free.

Lefferts Homestead

Address: Flatbush Avenue, Prospect Park, Brooklyn
Phone: 718-965-6505 • Ideal Age Group: 6 to 12
Admission: Free

I n a city built predominantly of steel, concrete, and chrome it's completely incongruous to see an old wooden farmhouse. The clapboard Lefferts Homestead was built a year after America declared its independence (1777), and it vibrates with Colonial history. Call for a complete listing of educational and entertaining activities specifically designed for children, most having a Colonial theme—creating old-fashioned toys and puppets, art projects using natural materials, or fashioning holiday ornaments using eighteenth-century techniques. The Dutch Colonial homestead is also located just steps from the renovated Prospect Park Wildlife Center, built to perfect child proportions and inhabited by the kind of pettable animals kids love. And before you go, make it a triple play by finishing the day not far away on the fabulously restored Prospect Park Carousel.

New York Firefighter's Friend

Address: 263 Lafayette Street bet. Prince and Spring Streets
Phone: 226-3142 • Ideal Age Group: 3 to 8
Admission: Free

If a visit to your neighborhood firehouse (see page 36) has ignited your child's interest in owning something, anything, NYFDish, your best bet is this SoHo specialty shop. Located a couple blocks from the department's medical center, your kids are likely to bump into a member of New York's Bravest shopping for his or her own fire-theme gifts. For adults they've got genuine recycled firemen's coats and insignia belt buckles, but the kids' gear is really hot. Store owner Nate Freedman carries plenty for fireman wannabes, including red plastic helmets, fire bears, toy fire trucks, and, of course, black-and-yellow fire uniforms that look regulation issue. If you like the popular T-shirt with FDNY on the front, and KEEP BACK 200 FT. on the flip side, you can pick them up here in navy, red, or white, sized for the whole family.

Police Academy Museum

Address: 235 East 20th Street bet. Second and Third Avenues • Phone: 477-9753
Ideal Age Group: 6 to 12 • Admission: Free

To kids, cops are cool. And at this east side NYPD academy, your children can rub holsters with police recruits training in the gym. They can also visit the second floor museum, where there's a wild collection of lethal-looking police weapons and weird bad guy stuff. Some of the memorabilia is boring (communications gear, police shields, whistles), but most of it is sensational—like the counterfeit money with brilliantly copied fives and twenties (I defy you to pick the fakes). There's also a case full of gangster "rub out" paraphernalia—sawed-off shotguns, ice picks, cement blackjacks, brass knuckles, even Al Capone's confiscated tommy gun. I was mesmerized by a bullet display from infamous shootings—the same caliber projectiles that killed JFK, Robert Kennedy, Martin Luther King, and John Lennon. Gruesome but gripping. If your kids want to take home a T-shirt with an authentic police insignia, visit the Second Avenue NYPD Accessories shop around the corner.

Pull Cart

**Address: 31 West 21st Street, 7th floor,
bet. Fifth and Sixth Avenues**
Phone: 727-7089 • Ideal Age Group: 4 to 12
Admission: Projects from $10

While plastercraft painting is popular with kids these days, Pull Cart offers something more—the permanence of quality ceramic ware. In a delightfully bright studio with south-facing windows, children and adults can select from more than ninety styles of earthenware mugs, teacups, plates, vases, bowls, napkin rings, and candlesticks. The white bisque has been fired once, and after you've painted or sponged on your decorations (more than seventy-five colors available), Pull Cart does a final firing. You can pick up the finished piece a few days later, which may be a drawback—delayed gratification is a bummer for kids. Nevertheless, the glazing technique is simple and fun, and for the uninitiated Pull Cart places easy-to-understand, laminated instructions at every flower-adorned, wooden worktable. This is a wonderful, do-it-yourself way for children to make a lasting and practical Mother's or Father's Day gift for about the cost of a week's allowance.

Speedway 17

Address: Route 17 North, Upper Saddle River, New Jersey
Phone: 201-934-1100 • Ideal Age Group: 4 to 12
Admission: $5 for license and goggles, $5 for 10 laps

Every few months you hear about a five-year-old taking the family station wagon out for a spin. That's because the urge to drive hits kids early. Out at Speedway 17—a short thirty minutes from the George Washington Bridge—they've converted an indoor tennis club into a go-cart raceway, and quenched every child's thirst to drive fast. Okay, speed is relative, but these electric (for ages four to eight) and propane-fueled racers (for ages eight and up) zip right along, promising a high thrill factor for aspiring Indy drivers. On one of two oval tracks, kids can get behind the wheel of a minicar and sprint around the loop, a lighted scoreboard recording laps. Track monitors are watching constantly, and the tip-proof cars have big bumper guards so it's all quite safe. The best part of the experience may be the laminated driver's license (with photo) and racing goggles that are issued to all first-time racers. Very cool and your kids get to keep them.

Wollman Rink

Address: Central Park at 63rd Street
Phone: 396-1010 • Ideal Age Group: 5 to 12
Admission: $7 adult/$3.50 children; $3.50 skate rental

The Sky Rink and Roller Blading venues at Chelsea Piers (see page 24) are exceptional, the Rockefeller Center Rink is famous, but if you want an unforgettable New York experience you've got to take the kids ice-skating in Central Park. The best place to do that is at the Wollman Rink where there's lots of open sky overhead, trees all around, and the great hotels of Central Park South casting afternoon shadows over the rolling lawns. This skyline view is so breathtaking even children stop their lazy loops to look up and stare. If you don't mind entering the park on winter evenings, come when the glittering lights of the surrounding buildings add to the fantasy feeling. In the summer, Wollman opens for in-line skating and roller skating, but who would pay to do this with miles of meandering pathways available in the park? Save the Wollman Rink for the heavy sweater days of fall and winter.

Notes

_____

_____

_____

_____

_____

_____

_____

_____

_____

_____

_____

_____

_____

_____

Notes

_____

_____

_____

_____

_____

_____

_____

_____

_____

_____

_____

_____

_____

_____

_____

_____

_____

Notes

About the Author

Allan Ishac is an advertising copywriter and creator of the Telly Award-winning Hard Hat Harry™ video series for children. He is a recipient of the Mayor's Volunteer Superstars Award for his bedtime story readings at Beth Israel Hospital in Manhattan and is also the author of *New York's 50 Best Places to Find Peace and Quiet*. He lives right here in this giant theme park—New York City.

About the Illustrator

Katherine Schultz is very fond of New York City. She lived here for five years and worked as a senior artist for the Children's Television Workshop. Katherine lives in Philadelphia where she is earning her master's degree in art education from the University of the Arts.